Better Homes and Gardens®

CHRISTMAS QUILTS & AFGHANS

BETTER HOMES AND GARDENS® BOOKS

Editor: Gerald M. Knox
Art Director: Ernest Shelton
Managing Editor: David A. Kirchner
Project Editors: James D. Blume, Marsha Jahns,
Project Managers: Liz Anderson,
    Jennifer Speer Ramundt, Angela K. Renkoski

Crafts Editor: Sara Jane Treinen
Senior Crafts Editors: Beverly Rivers, Patricia Wilens
Associate Crafts Editor: Nancy Reames

Associate Art Directors: Neoma Thomas,
    Linda Ford Vermie, Randall Yontz
Assistant Art Directors: Lynda Haupert,
    Harijs Priekulis, Tom Wegner
Graphic Designers: Mary Schlueter Bendgen,
    Michael Burns, Brenda Drake Lesch
Art Production: Director, John Berg;
    Associate, Joe Heuer;
    Office Manager, Michaela Lester

President, Book Group: Jeramy Lanigan
Vice President, Retail Marketing: Jamie L. Martin
Vice President, Administrative Services: Rick Rundall

BETTER HOMES AND GARDENS® MAGAZINE
President, Magazine Group: James A. Autry
Editorial Director: Doris Eby

MEREDITH CORPORATION OFFICERS
Chairman of the Executive Committee: E. T. Meredith III
Chairman of the Board: Robert A. Burnett
President: Jack D. Rehm

Christmas Quilts and Afghans
Editor: Nancy Reames
Contributing Editor: Colleen Bragg
Project Manager: Jennifer Speer Ramundt
Graphic Designer: Brenda Drake Lesch
Contributing Graphic Designer: Patricia Konecny
Contributing Illustrator: Chris Neubauer
Electronic Text Processor: Paula Forest

Cover projects: See pages 8, 20, and 38.

CONTENTS

Christmas Trees
A Stitching Celebration ———————— 4

Here's a festival of five tree projects to trim your home at Christmas and all through the year. There's a pine tree quilt, three knitted afghans, and an oversize "country" table runner with easy machine-appliqué instructions.

A Child's Fantasy
The Night Before Christmas ———————— 18

Children will delight in the wonders of Christmas with these four projects. Have you ever seen bunnies trimming the Christmas tree? Our knitted bunny afghan will thrill anyone. Other projects include a Santa crib quilt, a fabric Advent calendar, and a knitted afghan that depicts Santa and his reindeer team on Christmas Eve.

Star Dazzlers
To Brighten the Season ———————— 36

The projects in this chapter will excite both you and the lucky recipients of your handiwork. There's a wall hanging with four coordinating pillows, a knitted star and snowflake afghan, and a Christmas stocking. There's a quilted tree skirt with matching ornaments that will make your tree look festive even after all the gifts are gone. And for crocheters, there's a granny-style afghan with a star motif.

All Red and Wonderful
A Garden of Poinsettias ———————— 52

Don't you wish you could enjoy the beauty of the poinsettia flower throughout the year? The three projects in this chapter give you that chance. The poinsettia quilt is appliquéd with the bright red flowers. There's a crocheted afghan-stitch throw with holly and poinsettia panels, and an appliquéd quilt miniature that makes a cheery centerpiece or wall hanging.

Festive Gifts
To Enjoy Year-Round ———————— 62

Everyone enjoys handmade gifts. In this chapter there are seven fabulous ideas for gifts to make for your family and friends. Projects include a bright pink and green quilt, a wonderful quilted table runner, and some crocheted and knitted afghans that will be used for years to come.

Acknowledgments ———————— 80

CHRISTMAS TREES

A STITCHING CELEBRATION

Tall, stately, and beautiful in its simplicity, the Christmas tree is among the most splendid motifs for all manner of holiday handmades. Whether they're carefully stitched to fashion a quilt top or knitted around the edge of an afghan, the Christmas tree designs in this chapter most certainly will enhance your seasonal decorations.

The real joy of holiday decorating comes in finding special ways to set a festive mood in every room. You can bring a touch of Christmas cheer into the bedroom—and showcase your stitchery skills at the same time—by making a handsome holiday quilt.

Made from muslin and two shades of solid green cotton fabric, the tidy grove of unadorned evergreens is carefully plotted across the top of the 72x84-inch Christmas coverlet, *left.* Pieced into 72 squares and assembled in diagonal rows to complete the top, this lavishly quilted pine tree quilt is a true labor of love, destined to become a family heirloom.

You even can create a pretty bed covering of pine trees with a variety of cotton prints. Use red and green fabric scraps to stitch a quilt that captures the spirit of Christmas equally as well as the one we show.

For a quilt you'll be proud to display all year long, choose fabric prints in a wide range of colors or in one or two shades that complement your bedroom decor. Whatever your choice of fabrics, plan to cut three pine trees from each ⅛ yard of fabric.

Instructions for all projects in this chapter begin on page 10.

Seed stitches and a mosaic knitted Christmas tree border accent the 48½x72-inch afghan, *above*. Crocheted periwinkle blue puffs (that are added after the knitting is completed) decorate each tree. The center panel is knitted separately in stockinette stitches.

Curl up on Christmas morn with a cozy knitted 48x60-inch afghan, *opposite*, patterned with eyelet and cabled pine tree squares. To make this afghan extra-special, choose a fluffy yarn in your favorite pastel.

Bordered with festive holiday motifs, the beautifully colored 48x60-inch afghan, *opposite,* features a center panel of moss stitches and cables. Worked in worsted-weight yarns, it can be knit all in one piece using circular needles.

Homespun red and green plaid fabrics create the oversized table runner, *above.* Two big hearts and an assortment of tree shapes and sizes are machine-appliquéd to a brown-and-white windowpane-checked fabric.

Our cloth measures 23x65 inches, but you easily can adapt the pattern to fit the size of your table.

Pine Tree Quilt

Shown on pages 4 and 5.

Quilt measures 72x84 inches.

MATERIALS
9¾ yards muslin (includes
    backing)
3¾ yards green fabric for trees
    (To make a scrap quilt, plan
    to cut three trees from each ⅛
    yard of fabric.)
1 yard matching green binding
    fabric
¼ yard dark green for trunks
Quilt batting
Quilting thread and needle
Cardboard or template plastic
Ruler
Rotary cutter and mat (optional)

INSTRUCTIONS
    CUTTING: Cut and set aside
two 37x88-inch muslin pieces for
backing.
    From green tree fabric, cut six
9½-inch squares and two 7-inch
squares. Cut each in half *diagonally* to make 16 triangles. Set
these aside for assembly.
    Trace patterns A–K, *right and
opposite,* onto template material.
These patterns include ¼-inch
seam allowances. Cut out all templates. Trace around templates
onto the wrong side of the appropriate fabrics as follows: From
green tree fabric, mark and cut
77 each of templates A, B, and D;
cut 154 of Template C. From
muslin, mark and cut 154 each of
templates G, H, I, J and K; cut 231
of Template F. From dark green,
cut 77 of Template E.

    TREE BLOCKS: Referring to
the Block Diagram on page 12,
make 72 complete tree blocks.
Make five half blocks (tree top)
with tree pieces A, B, and C and
muslin pieces I, J, and K. Make
five half blocks (tree bottom) with
tree pieces C, D, and E and muslin
pieces F, G, and H.

continued

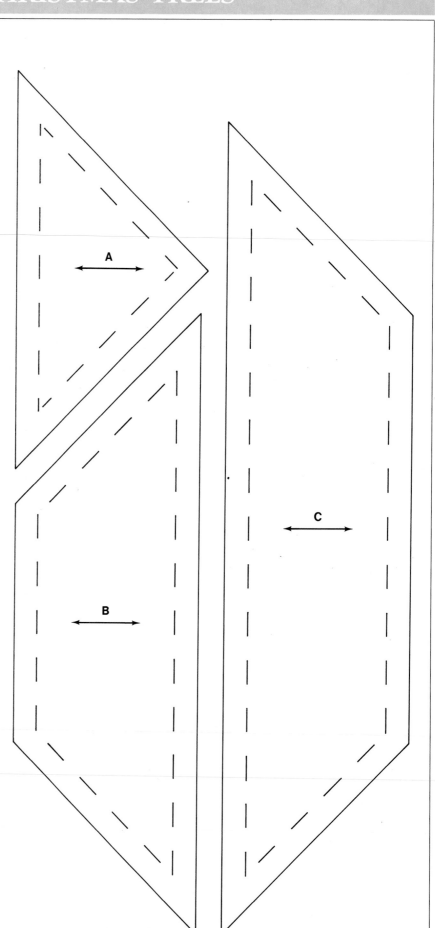

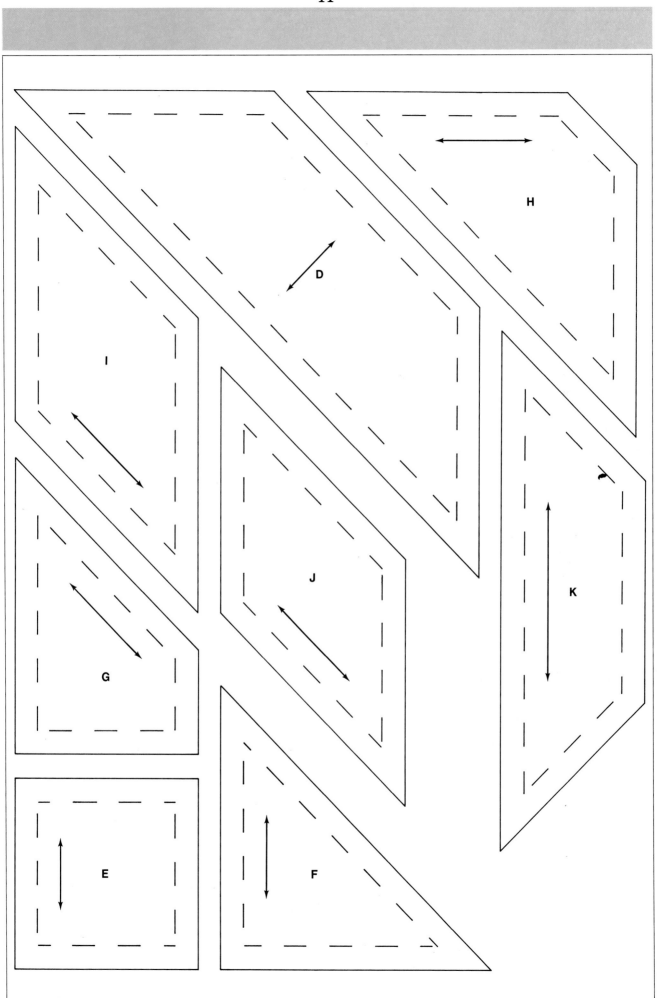

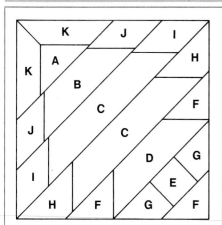

Block Diagram

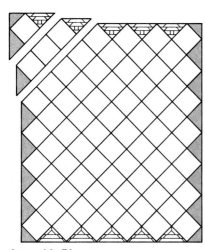

Assembly Diagram
PINE TREE QUILT

ASSEMBLY: Refer to Assembly Diagram, *above*, and lay out the completed blocks on a floor or table. The 16 green triangles are positioned at the sides and corners, and the tree half blocks are positioned at top and bottom.

Starting at one corner, assemble blocks and triangles into diagonal rows. Then assemble rows to complete the quilt top.

QUILTING: Use ¼-inch seams to sew backing fabric together to make one 73½x88-inch piece. Lay backing flat, wrong side up, and layer batting on top of it. Center quilt top on batting. Baste all three layers together, starting at the center and working out to the edges. Quilt as desired. The quilt shown on pages 4 and 5 features outline quilting ¼ inch inside each seam line. When quilting is complete, remove basting. Trim batting and backing even with quilt top.

BINDING: Cut the green binding fabric into 2½-inch-wide bias strips. Sew strips together, with right sides facing, to make a bias strip length that measures approximately 320 inches. Press the binding in half lengthwise, wrong sides together.

Starting at the center of any quilt side, stitch binding to right side of quilt using ¼-inch seams and overlapping the binding edges ½ inch at the starting point. Turn binding over the raw edge; hand-sew to backing.

Mosaic Christmas Tree Afghan

Shown on page 6.

Afghan measures approximately 48½x71 inches.

MATERIALS
Brunswick Germantown knitting worsted (100-gram skein): 11 skeins white sand (4001), 2 skeins *each* of Irish green (4008) and fuchsia (4041), and 1 skein periwinkle blue (401)
Sizes 7 and 8 circular 36-inch knitting needles, or size to obtain gauge given below
Two 6-inch-long stitch holders
Size 8 knitting needles
Size 4 knitting needles
Size K crochet hook
Tapestry needle

Abbreviations: See page 15.
Gauge: 5 sts = 1 inch and 7 rows = 1 inch in st st on Size 7 needles; 5 sts = 1 inch in mosaic st on Size 8 needles.

INSTRUCTIONS
BEGINNING BORDER: Using Size 8 circular needles and white yarn, cast on 245 sts.
Note: Mosaic knitting is a garter and sl st pat using two yarn colors. In this afghan 2 rows of green alternate with 2 rows of white. The tree motif is created by slipping sts. Always sl sts as if to p and leave the yarn in back of the sl sts on the right-side rows and in front of the sl sts on the wrong-

side rows. Each row on the Tree Chart, *opposite*, represents 2 rows of knitting. When working the tree motifs on the *right side* of the afghan, follow the chart to determine the knitted and slipped sts. On the *wrong side* rows, *always* k and sl the same sts as the previous row.

On every row that *begins* and *ends* with green yarn, k all green stitches and sl the blank square (white) sts. On every row that *begins* and *ends* with a blank square, k all the blank squares with the white yarn and sl the black square (green) sts.

Row 1: Referring to chart, k 1; rep bet A–B 11 times; end k 2 with green.
Row 2: K all green sts with green and sl all white sts.
Row 3: Referring to chart, k all white squares with white and sl all green sts, k 1, rep bet A–B 11 times; end k 2 with white.
Row 4: With white yarn, k all white sts and sl all green sts.
Rows 5–42: Continue to work from chart as established. Fasten off green yarn at end of Row 42.
Row 43: Working from chart, k with white yarn and sl green sts.
Row 44 (wrong side): With the white yarn, k white sts and sl green sts. Place first 25 sts onto st holder. Complete row and place last 25 sts onto st holder. Fasten off white yarn—195 sts on needle.

CENTER OF AFGHAN: *Row 45:* Join white yarn and using Size 7 needles, k 1; * p 1, k 1; rep from * across—195 sts.
Row 46: K 1, * p 1, k 1; rep from * across.
Rows 47–58: Rep Row 46—14 rows of seed st pat established.
Row 59: Work seed st over 11 sts, k 173, seed st over last 11 sts.
Row 60: Work seed st over 11 sts, p 173 sts, work seed st over last 11 sts.

Rep rows 59 and 60 until center measures 57 inches beyond 14 rows of seed st (Row 58). Leave sts on needles.

RIGHT BORDER: With Size 8 needles, work the Tree Chart pattern over the 25 sts on st holder. Rep rows 1–44 five times—six

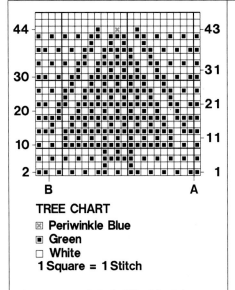

TREE CHART
- ⊠ **Periwinkle Blue**
- ▣ **Green**
- ☐ **White**

1 Square = 1 Stitch

trees completed. Working in reverse order, work the chart from rows 42–1 one time; then rep rows 44–1 four times—five upside-down trees. Place sts on holder. Rep right border on left border sts.

SEWING BORDERS: With white yarn on tapestry needle and right sides facing, sew side borders to the center. To keep work lying flat, sew through the single strand of the edge sts along both pieces. The border strips will be longer than the center portion. Estimate the number of rows in the center portion required to equal the length of the side borders plus the 14 rows of seed st.

Work the center portion in st st and seed st pats until work equals the length of the borders minus the 14 rows of seed st. Then work the seed st pat for 14 rows. When seed st pat is completed, sew borders to the center.

END BORDER: Using Size 8 circular needle, work across all 245 sts (includes 25 sts on st holders at both sides) following chart from rows 44–1.

Note: On Row 44, you sl *all white sts* where you are supposed to sl green sts. The green sts will be added with duplicate sts after the border is complete. Fasten off green yarn at end of Row 1. Bind off loosely in white. Cut a 2-yard strand of green yarn and work duplicate sts (see page 14) over the slipped white sts of Row 44.

Refer to Tree Chart for placement. Weave the yarn on the back side of the row as you stitch.

BIAS BINDING: With Size 4 needles and fuchsia yarn, cast on 8 sts.
Row 1: P.
Row 2: K 1, **k in front and back of next st—inc made;** k 4, k 2 tog.
Row 3: P.
Rep rows 2 and 3 until length of binding fits around afghan. Do not bind off sts.
Sew one side of binding completely around the right side of afghan; sew into only one st of mosaic tree border. Add or subtract rows until binding edges meet; bind off.
Sew binding to the wrong side of afghan.

CROCHETED TREE TOPS: Referring to the Tree Chart, locate the blue X at the top of the tree and the corresponding place on the afghan. With crochet hook, **draw blue yarn through to right side at center of tree top, ch 4, (yo, draw up lp in same st, yo, draw through 2 lps on hook) 4 times—5 lps on hook; insert hook in st 3 rows above X st, draw lp through st and the 5 lps on hook—puff made and fastened to afghan;** fasten off. Draw yarn to back side and weave in ends. Rep the crocheted puffs above each tree.

FINISHING: Weave in ends. Block afghan to size.

Pink Cabled Pine Tree Afghan

Shown on page 7.

Afghan measures 48x60 inches.

MATERIALS
Reynolds Kitten (50 gram skein): 12 skeins pink (99)
Size 9 circular knitting needles, or size to obtain gauge given below
Cable needle
Stitch markers (optional)
Tapestry needle

Abbreviations: See page 15.
Gauge: 4 sts = 1 inch in st st.

INSTRUCTIONS
PINE TREE (over 28 sts):
Row 1: P.
Row 2: K.
Rows 3, 5, and 7: P 13, k 2, p 13.
Rows 4, 6, and 8: K 13, p 2, k 13.
Rows 9 and 11: P 2, k 2, (p 4, k 4) 2 times, p 4, k 2, p 2.
Rows 10 and 12: K 2, p 2, (k 4, p 4) 2 times, k 4, p 2, k 2.
Row 13: P 2, sl 2 to cn, hold in front of work, p 2, k 2 from cn, p 2, sl 2 to cn, hold in back of work, k 2, k 2 from cn, p 4, sl 2 to cn, hold in front of work, k 2, k 2 from cn, p 2, sl 2 to cn, hold in back, k 2, p 2 from cn, p 2.
Rows 14 and 16: K 4, p 2, k 2, p 4, k 4, p 4, k 2, p 2, k 4.
Row 15: P 4, k 2, p 2, k 4, p 4, k 4, p 2, k 2, p 4.
Row 17: P 4, sl 2 to cn, hold in front of work, p 1, k 2 from cn, sl 1 to cn, hold in back of work, k 2, p 1 from cn, sl 2 to cn, hold in front of work, p 2, k 2 from cn, sl 2 to cn, hold in back of work, k 2, p 2 from cn, sl 2 to cn, hold in front of work, p 1, k 2 from cn, sl 1 to cn, hold in back of work, k 2, p 1 from cn, p 4.
Rows 18 and 20: K 6, p 2, k 4, p 4, k 4, p 2, k 6.
Row 19: P 6, k 2, p 4, sl 2 to cn, hold in back of work, k 2, k 2 from cn, p 4, k 2, p 6.
Row 21: P 6, sl 2 to cn, hold in front of work, p 2, k 2 from cn, p 2, k 4, p 2, sl 2 to cn, hold in back of work, k 2, p 2 from cn, p 6.
Rows 22 and 24: K 8, p 2, k 2, p 4, k 2, p 2, k 8.
Row 23: P 8, k 2, p 2, sl 2 to cn, hold in back of work, k 2, k 2 from cn, p 2, k 2, p 8.
Row 25: P 8, (sl 2 to cn, hold in front of work, p 1, k 2 from cn, sl 1 to cn, hold in back of work, k 2, p 1 from cn) 2 times, p 8.
Rows 26 and 28: K 10, p 2, k 4, p 2, k 10.
Row 27: P 10, k 2, p 4, k 2, p 10.
Row 29: P 10, sl 2 to cn, hold in front of work, p 1, k 2, from cn, p 2, sl 1 to cn, hold in back of work, k 2, p 1 from cn, p 10.

continued

Rows 30 and 32: K 11, p 2, k 2, p 2, k 11.

Row 31: P 11, k 2, p 2, k 2, p 11.

Row 33: P 11, sl 2 to cn, hold in front of work, p 1, k 2 from cn, sl 1 to cn, hold in back of work, k 2, p 1 from cn, p 11.

Rows 34 and 36: K 12, p 4, k 12.

Row 35: P 12, sl 2 to cn, hold in back of work, k 2, k 2 from cn, p 12.

Row 37: P.
Row 38: K.

EYELET (over 28 sts):
Rows 1 and 3: K.
Rows 2 and 4: P.
Row 5: * K 2 tog, yo; rep from *, end k 2.
Row 6: K.
Rows 7–10: Rep rows 1–4.
Row 11: K 2, * yo, k 2 tog; rep from *.
Row 12: K.
Rows 13–36: Rep rows 1–12 two times more.
Row 37: K.
Row 38: P.

AFGHAN: Cast on 190 sts. Work in garter st (k every row) for 1 inch. Inc 16 sts evenly spaced over last row—206 sts. *Note:* Use stitch markers to separate the different pattern areas, if desired.

Next row: (right side) Work garter st over 5 sts, * work Row 1 of Pine Tree over next 28 sts, work Row 1 of Eyelet over next 28 sts; rep from * two times more; work Pine Tree over next 28 sts; garter st over last 5 sts.

Keeping 5 garter sts at each end, work rows 2–38 of Pine Tree and Eyelet pats.

Next row: (right side) Garter st over 5 sts, then * work Row 1 of Eyelet over next 28 sts, work Row 1 of Pine Tree over next 28 sts; rep from * two times more; work Eyelet over next 28 sts; garter st over last 5 sts.

Continue to work alternate 38 row pats as established until afghan measures approximately 60 inches from beginning. Work should end when last row of the ninth set of pats is completed. Dec 16 sts evenly spaced across last row—190 sts. Work in garter st for 1 inch. Bind off all sts.

Use tapestry needle to weave in ends; carefully block to shape.

Heart and Tree Bordered Afghan

Shown on page 8.

Afghan measures 48x60 inches.

MATERIALS
Bernat Berella 4 (100-gram skein): 2 skeins scarlet (8933), 3 skeins natural (8940), and 8 skeins stormy teal (8988)
Size 8 circular 36-inch needle or size to obtain gauge given below
Cable needle
Tapestry needle
Stitch markers; bobbins

Abbreviations: See page 15.
Gauge: 4.5 sts = 1 inch in st st.

INSTRUCTIONS
MOSS STITCH (over even number of sts): *Row 1:* * K 1, p 1, rep from *.
Rows 2 and 3: * P 1, k 1, rep from *.
Row 4: * K 1, p 1 rep from *.
Rep rows 1–4 for pat.
Note: For uneven number of sts:
Rows 1 and 2: * K 1, p 1; rep from *; end k 1.
Rows 3 and 4: * P 1, k 1; rep from *; end p 1.

CABLE (over 6 sts):
Row 1: K 6.
Rows 2, 4, 6, and 8: P 6.
Row 3: Sl 3 sts to cn, hold in back of work, k 3, k 3 from cn.
Rows 5 and 7: K 6.
Rep rows 1–8 rows for pat.

CENTER PATTERN (over 176 sts): *Rows 1–4:* Work in Moss Stitch.

Row 5: Work Row 1 of Moss Stitch over 4 sts, place marker, (work Row 1 of Cable over next 6 sts, place marker, work Moss Stitch over next 21 sts, place marker) 6 times, work Cable over next 6 sts, place marker, work Moss Stitch over next 4 sts.

Row 6: Work Row 2 of Moss Stitch and Row 2 of Cable over the appropriate sts, slipping markers as you work.

Rows 7–12: Continue to work moss st (rows 1–4) and cable pats (rows 3–8) for the center panel.

AFGHAN: With scarlet, cast on 206 sts. Work in moss st pat for 1 inch; inc 15 sts evenly spaced across last row—221 sts.

Row 1 (right side): Continuing in moss st pat, work first 6 sts with scarlet. Join natural and k 209 sts; attach a second ball of scarlet and work rem 6 sts in moss st pat.

Row 2 (wrong side): Work first 6 sts in moss st pat with scarlet; p 209 sts with natural; work last 6 sts in moss st pat with A.

Rows 3 and 4: Rep rows 1 and 2.

Row 5: Wind 7 bobbins with scarlet and 6 bobbins with teal. Keeping to moss st pat on 6 sts of each edge, and to st st pat on center 209 sts, work from Chart 1, *opposite,* as follows: When work-

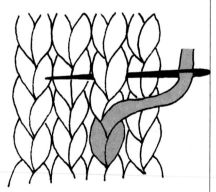

DUPLICATE STITCH

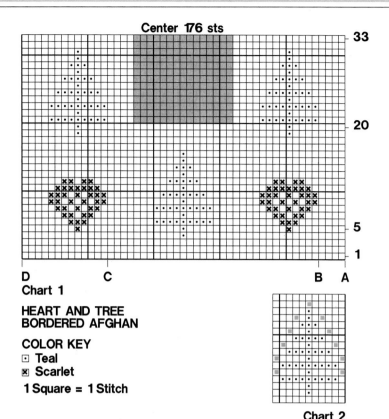

Center 176 sts

— 33

— 20

— 5

— 1

D   C   B A

Chart 1

**HEART AND TREE
BORDERED AFGHAN**

COLOR KEY
☐ Teal
☒ Scarlet
1 Square = 1 Stitch

Chart 2

ing on *right side rows,* work from A to C over 36 sts; rep between B and C five times; then work 13 sts between C and D.

Row 6: When working on *wrong side rows,* work from D to B over 45 sts; rep 32 sts between C and B five times; then work 4 sts between B and A.

Rows 7–19: Continue in moss and st st pats following same chart.

Row 20: With wrong side fac-

ing, continue to work 6 sts in moss st pat with scarlet; work border pat in st st from Chart 1 over next 17 sts; p across next 175 sts with teal (inc 1 st in center of 175 sts—176 sts); work border pat in st st from Chart 1 over next 17 sts, then work moss st pat with scarlet on last 6 sts—222 sts.

Rows 21–24: Continue to work 6 sts in moss st with scarlet; work 17 sts in st st following Chart 1;

work Center Pattern, *opposite,* over 176 sts with teal, then work 17 sts in st st following Chart 1; work 6 sts in moss st pat with scarlet.

Row 25: Work 6 sts in moss st pat with scarlet; work 17 sts in st st following Chart 1; work Row 5 of Center Pattern over 176 sts with teal, then work 17 sts in st st following Chart 1; work last 6 sts in moss st pat with scarlet.

Continue to work as established; rep rows 1–33 of Chart 1 for 17 st side border, eight times more, alternating the trees and hearts, and spacing 7 rows of natural between motifs. Continue working rows 5–12 of Center Pattern over center 176 sts.

Begin a 10th tree of Chart 1 border, working until length measures approximately 56 inches from beg and the tree motifs are worked to within 4 rows of completion on each side. Work 4 rows of moss st pat over center 176 sts with teal while completing last 4 rows of trees. Fasten off natural. Beg to work complete border pat over total 210 sts from Chart 1 (Row 1), dec 1 st in center of afghan on first row—221 sts including 12 red side sts. Complete border. With right side facing, k across with scarlet, evenly dec 15 sts—206 sts. Work moss st pat for 1 inch. Bind off.

Duplicate st the red sts (marked with a blue square on Chart 2, *left*) around the trees. Weave in ends. Block the afghan.

Knitting and Crocheting Abbreviations

beg	begin(ning)
bl	block
CC	contrasting color
ch	chain
cl	cluster
cn	cable needle
dc	double crochet
dec	decrease
dpn	double-pointed needles
dtr	double treble crochet
grp	group
hdc	half-double crochet
inc	increase

k	knit
LH	left hand
lp(s)	loop(s)
MC	main color
p	purl
pat(s)	pattern(s)
pc	popcorn
psso	pass sl st over
rem	remaining
rep	repeat
RH	right hand
rnd(s)	round(s)
sc	single crochet

sk	skip
sl st	slip stitch
sp	space
st(s)	stitch(es)
st st	stockinette stitch
tbl	through back loop
tog	together
trc	treble crochet
yo	yarn over
*	repeat from * as indicated
( )	repeat between ( ) as indicated
[ ]	repeat between [ ] as indicated

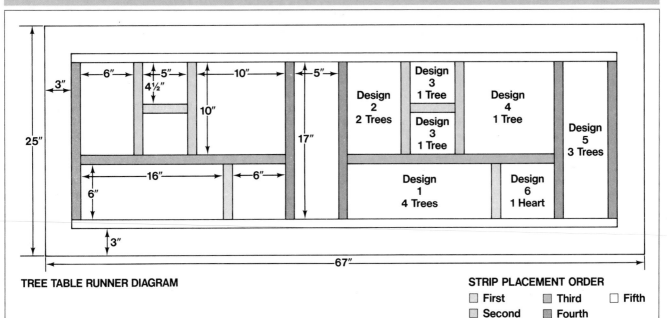

TREE TABLE RUNNER DIAGRAM

STRIP PLACEMENT ORDER
- ☐ First
- ☐ Second
- ■ Third
- ■ Fourth
- ☐ Fifth

Tree Table Runner

Shown on page 9.

Runner measures 23x65 inches.

MATERIALS
2 yards beige cotton plaid
  background fabric
2 yards fleece
2 yards small red check fabric
  (for strips, backing, and trees)
1 yard of red and green plaid
  fabric (for pleated ruffle and
  trees)
¼ yard *each* of three different
  red and green check or plaid
  fabrics
2½ yards 17-inch-wide fusible
  webbing paper
Sewing thread in shades of red
  and green
Transparent nylon thread
Typing paper; tracing paper

INSTRUCTIONS
Note: Fabrics should measure
at least 45 inches wide.
Cut 1-inch-wide strips of fusible webbing paper into the following lengths: five 17½-inch
strips, four 10½-inch strips, and
two *each* of 61-, 5½-, 6½-, and
23½-inch strips.

Referring to the patterns, *opposite,* trace eight Design 1 trees,
two Design 4 trees, four *each* Design 2 and 3 trees, six Design 5
trees, and two Design 6 hearts
onto remaining fusible webbing
paper; cut out shapes.

PREPARING THE APPLIQUÉ
STRIPS: Cut one 25x67-inch
rectangle for the runner backing
from red check fabric; set aside.
Fuse the 1-inch webbing strips
to the wrong side of the remaining piece of red check fabric. Set
any leftover fabric aside for cutting tree shapes. Cut the fabric
into 1-inch strips along the webbing markings.
Cut nine 2½x45-inch strips of
red and green plaid fabric; seam
strips together along short sides.
Press in half lengthwise, wrong
sides facing. Set aside for the ruffle. Set remaining fabric aside for
tree or heart shapes.
Fuse webbing tree and heart
shapes to assorted fabrics. For
added interest, fuse some shapes
on the fabric bias, if desired. Cut
shapes from fabric.
Cut a 25x67-inch rectangle
from the background plaid. Referring to the Table Runner Diagram, *above,* for placement, pin
then fuse the red checked strips

to the background. Follow the
placement order indicated on the
diagram to ensure the raw edges
of the center strips are covered.
Referring to the photo on page
9 and following the tree and heart
placement on the diagram, fuse
the tree and heart shapes to the
runner top. Repeat right side designs in the same spaces on the
left side of the runner.

APPLIQUÉING: Cut a 25x67-
inch rectangle from the fleece and
baste it to the wrong side of the
runner top. Machine-satin-stitch
over edges of all strips using red
thread. Use typing paper under
the fleece to avoid stretching the
fabric when sewing. Machine-satin-stitch around tree and heart
shapes using the red and green
threads.

FINISHING: Gather ruffle to fit
around runner. With right sides
facing and using ½-inch seams,
sew ruffle to runner.
With right sides facing, sew
backing to top, leaving an opening for turning. Trim seam allowance and clip curves; turn and
press. Sew opening closed.
Using the nylon thread, tack
through all layers at corners of
each rectangle.

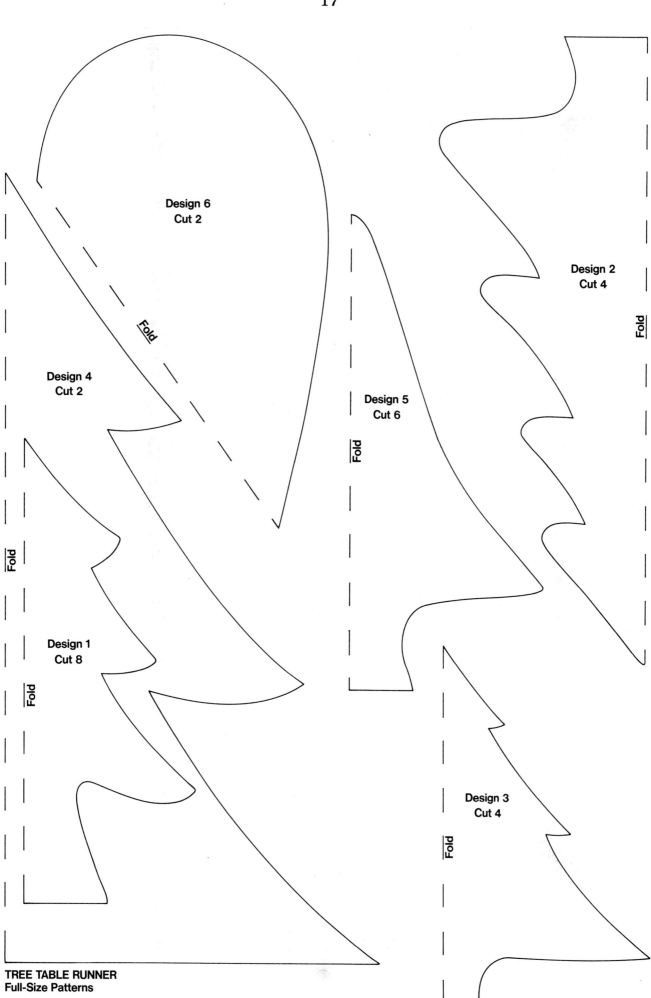

Design 6
Cut 2

Design 4
Cut 2

Fold

Design 2
Cut 4

Fold

Design 5
Cut 6

Fold

Fold

Design 1
Cut 8

Fold

Design 3
Cut 4

Fold

TREE TABLE RUNNER
Full-Size Patterns

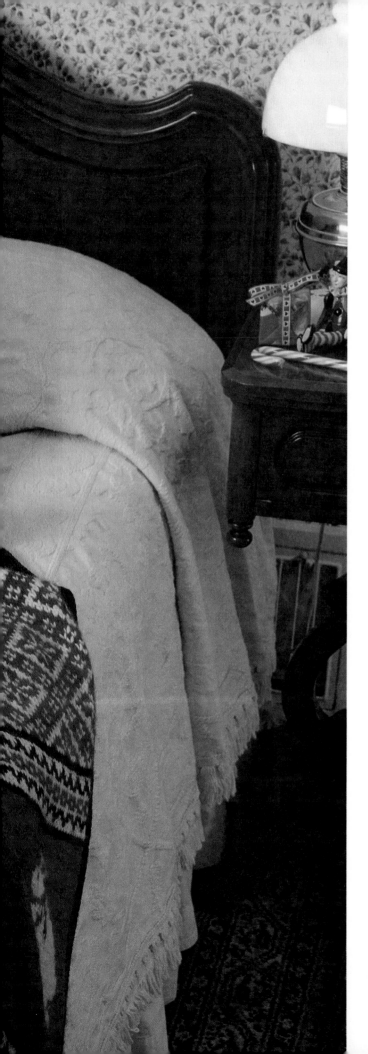

THE NIGHT BEFORE CHRISTMAS

♦ ♦ ♦

A child's joy at Christmastime resounds the wonder of the season. The magic of wonderful things makes eyes light up and cheeks glow with anticipation. And just imagine a child's delight with an afghan or quilt that's been stitched especially for this enchanting time of the year! This chapter includes child-pleasing projects that will appeal to all who are young at heart.

As any parent knows, children dream of Christmas Day long before the actual holiday is at hand. For all those cold winter nights before Christmas, make a cozy afghan that's sure to keep kids warm in their beds.

Youngsters will love to cuddle up in this afghan, *left,* with its visions of a winter wonderland—drifting snowflakes, playful bunnies, and snow-laden evergreens. Experienced knitters will enjoy the intricacies of working with a variety of patterns and techniques.

The afghan is worked in stockinette stitches on circular needles. A simple crocheted border of slip stitches and single crochet edges the entire afghan.

Color changes are accomplished with one of two techniques. The Christmas tree, snow-flake, and geometric border designs employ the stranded knitting method—knit with one color and carry the other accordingly. To work the bunnies, use separate balls or bobbins of yarn for each motif.

Instructions for all projects in this chapter begin on page 24.

Lull a little one to sleep on Christmas Eve with the snuggly Santa Claus crib quilt, *opposite*. Patchwork squares and a hand-quilted border make up this captivating coverlet that also could be used as a seasonal wall hanging.

Delight youngsters who long to count the days till Christmas by making the quilted Advent calendar, *above*. The ruffled, three-dimensional tree is ornamented with delightful ceramic buttons that are hidden under the numbered packages until the appropriate days arrive.

At one time or another, every child hopes to catch a glimpse of Santa Claus as he goes about his business on Christmas Eve. This scenic portrayal of Santa's midnight ride, *above* and *right,* complete with miniature sleigh and eight tiny reindeer, captures the essence of a child's Christmas fantasy. Knit this wintry afghan in a beautiful shade of copen blue and ecru knitting worsted. Worked in one piece on circular needles, the afghan measures 46x58 inches.

Chart 2

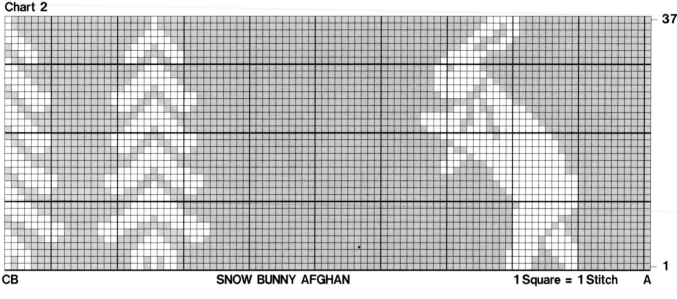

CB   SNOW BUNNY AFGHAN   1 Square = 1 Stitch   A

Chart 1

Chart 3

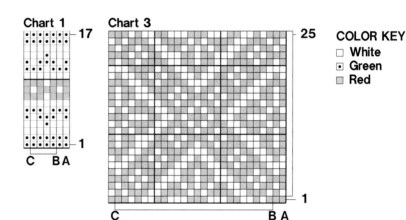

C   B A

C   B A

COLOR KEY

☐ White
⊡ Green
▨ Red

Snow Bunny Afghan

Shown on pages 18 and 19.

Afghan measures 42x55 inches.

MATERIALS

Aarlan Cristal (50-gram ball): 10
 balls cranberry (4642), 7 balls
 off-white (4635), and 5 balls
 dark green (4699)
Size 8 circular 29-inch knitting
 needle or size to obtain gauge
 given below
Size 7 circular 29-inch knitting
 needle or size to obtain gauge
 given below
5 large knitting bobbins
 (optional)
Size G crochet hook or size to
 obtain gauge given below
Tapestry needle

Abbreviations: See page 15.
Gauge: With smaller needles in
 st st, 19 sts = 4 inches; 24
 rows = 4 inches. Use larger
 needles when working Chart
 3 to obtain same gauge. With
 crochet hook, 18 sc = 4
 inches.

INSTRUCTIONS

Note: The entire afghan is worked
in st st, except for the crocheted
border. Selvage sts are included
on both edges. Charts 1 and 3 are
worked using the stranded knitting method. To work Chart 2,
use separate balls or bobbins for
each motif. The background color
is worked with separate balls on
both sides of the bunnies; it is
carried and stranded behind the
tree designs. Always twist yarn
when changing colors to avoid
holes. For ease in working, you
may want to transfer the complete pattern of Chart 2 onto
graph paper to establish placement of the mirror image.

 Using smaller needles and
cranberry yarn, cast on 195 sts.
Work even in st st for 8 rows.

 Follow Chart 1, *above left,* for
17 rows using cranberry, dark
green, and off-white yarns. Work
from A–C once; rep from B–C 47
times more; end with one selvage
st. Rep the same stitching sequence on wrong side rows.

 Next 8 rows: Work even with
cranberry.

 Next 37 rows: Follow Chart 2,
above top, using cranberry and
off-white yarns. Follow the chart
by working from A–C then B–A
on right side rows. This reverses
the direction of the other bunny.
Rep the same stitching sequence
on wrong side rows.

 Next 8 rows: Work even with
cranberry.

Next 17 rows: Follow Chart 1 using cranberry, dark green, and off-white yarns.

Next 25 rows: Change to larger needles (if necessary for gauge) and using cranberry and off-white yarns, work Row 1 of Chart 3, *opposite.* Work from A–C once; rep from B–C 7 times; end row with one selvage st. Right and wrong sides are worked following the same stitching sequence. Complete rows 2–25.

Keeping to pat as established, work rows 2–25 of Chart 3 five times.

Next 17 rows: Change back to smaller needles and follow Chart 1 using cranberry, dark green, and off-white yarns.

Next 8 rows: Work even with cranberry.

Turn Chart 2 upside down.
Next 37 rows: Follow Chart 2 working rows 37–1.

Next 8 rows: Work even with cranberry.

Next 17 rows: Follow Chart 1 using cranberry, dark green, and off-white yarns.

Next 8 rows: Work even with cranberry. Bind off.

BORDER: *Rnd 1:* With right side of afghan facing, use dark green yarn and crochet hook to sl st evenly around afghan. Make sure work lies flat and the same number of sl sts are crocheted on opposite sides of the afghan; join to beg of rnd. *Do not turn.*

Rnd 2: Sc in each sl st around, working through center of each st and working 3 sc in each corner st; join with sl st to first sc; ch 1, turn.

Rnds 3–6: Sc in each sc around, working 3 sc in each corner st; join with sl st to sc at beg of rnd; ch 1, turn.

Rnd 7: Sl st in each sc around; join to first sc. Fasten off.

Weave in ends and carefully block afghan to size.

Continuous Bias Binding

Bias binding is probably the most common method for finishing the edges of quilts. True bias binding has a stretch that allows it to shape and curve smoothly around corners. It's this stretch that makes it a desirable edging for quilts and for appliqué projects that require bias-cut strips.

To make maximum use of one piece of fabric when cutting bias strips, follow the instructions and step-by-step diagrams *below.*

A 36-inch square of fabric will make enough 2- to 2½-inch-wide binding to go around most quilts. If you use the full width of the fabric, you will have plenty of binding. To make wider binding, you need to use more than one square of fabric and repeat the bias-making steps.

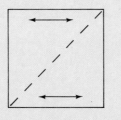

1 Referring to the drawing, *above,* cut a 36-inch square of fabric (or use the full fabric width), and draw a diagonal line from corner to corner. Cutting atop the diagonal line, split the square into two triangles.

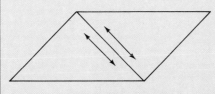

2 Using ¼-inch seams, sew the triangles together along the *crosswise* straight edges as shown in the drawing, *above.* Press the seam open.

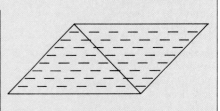

3 Referring to the drawing, *above,* use a pencil and ruler to draw horizontal rows the width of the bias binding plus the seam allowance.

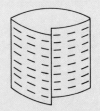

4 With right sides together, bring the diagonal ends of the piece together and offset the joining by one row or line. The drawing, *above,* shows the first marking on the right side matched with the top edge on the left side. Using a ¼-inch seam, sew the edges together to make a tube; press seams open. Cut the tube into a bias strip beginning at the top edge and the first joined marking on the tube. Cut through one thickness of fabric. Cut around and around along the pencil line to create one long strip of bias binding.

THE NIGHT BEFORE CHRISTMAS

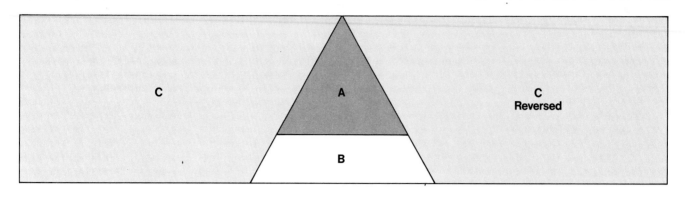

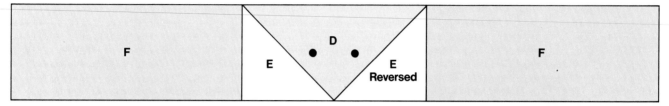

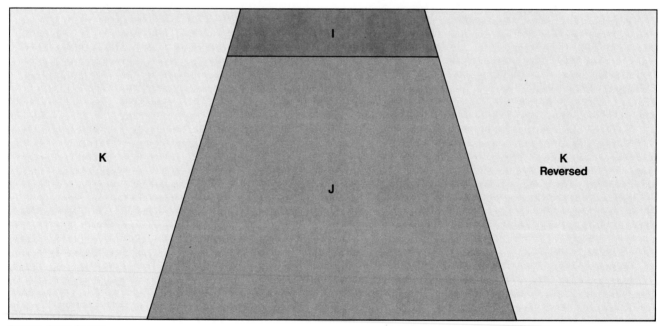

SANTA CRIB QUILT
Full-Size Patterns

COLOR KEY
☐ White
■ Black
☐ Pink
■ Red
☐ Tan

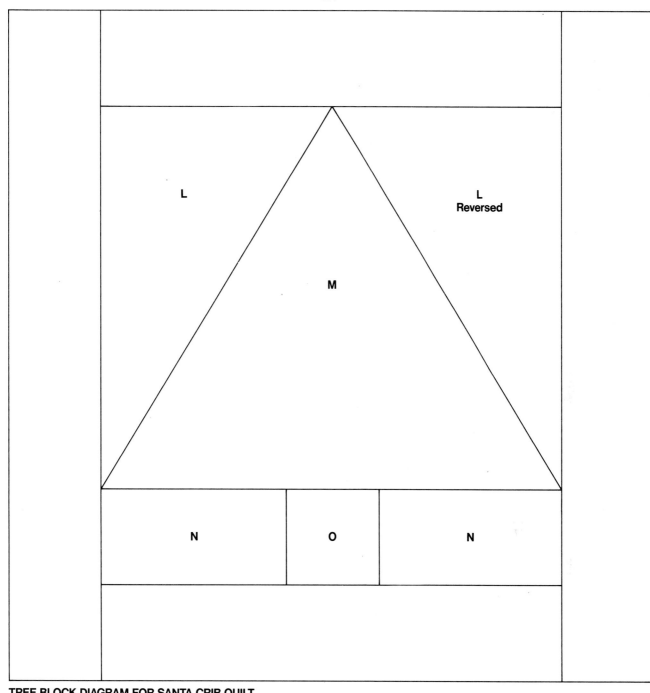

TREE BLOCK DIAGRAM FOR SANTA CRIB QUILT

Santa Crib Quilt

Shown on page 20.

Finished quilt is approximately 44x58 inches.

MATERIALS
1¾ yards tan print fabric for Santa background and outer border
1¾ yards backing fabric
1½ yards red fabric for Santa and inner border
⅝ yard dark green fabric for tree block borders
⅓ yard green fabric for trees
⅓ yard beige or tan solid fabric for tree backgrounds
⅛ yard of white or muslin fabric for beard, hat trim, and cuffs
⅛ yard *each* of brown, pink, and black fabrics for tree trunk, face, and belt
Nonpermanent marker
Quilt batting
Quilting thread and needle
Tracing paper
Cardboard or template plastic
Black embroidery floss

INSTRUCTIONS
Note: All seams are sewn with a ¼-inch seam allowance and with right sides of fabrics together.

TEMPLATES: Trace each full-size pattern, *above* and *opposite,* onto tracing paper. Transfer patterns to cardboard or template plastic, adding ¼-inch seam allowances to all pieces. Cut out all template patterns.

CUTTING: From the tan print fabric, cut two 4x60-inch side borders down the length of the
continued

yardage. Cut two border strips each 4x46 inches. From the remaining background fabric, cut pieces for the Santa blocks as follows: 18 *each* of templates C, C reversed, K, and K reversed; cut 36 each of templates F and G.

For the inner border, cut two 1½x50-inch strips of red fabric down the length of the yardage and two 1½x37-inch strips across the width of the fabric. For the binding, cut five 2¼x39-inch red strips crosswise. From the remaining red fabric, cut pieces for the Santa blocks as follows: 18 *each* of templates A, E, E reversed, and J; cut 36 template H.

To complete the Santa blocks, cut 18 of template I from the black fabric and 18 of template D from the pink fabric. From the white fabric, cut 18 *each* of templates B, E, E reversed, and D; cut 36 of template G.

For the tree block, cut 17 of template M from the tree fabric and 17 of template O from the brown fabric. From the tan background fabric, cut 17 *each* of template L and L reversed; cut 34 of template N. From green border fabric cut 34 strips each 1½x5½ inches and 34 strips each 1½x7½ inches for the borders.

BLOCKS: Assemble the Santa block in sections as shown on the pattern on page 26. Sew the sections together, matching seam lines carefully. Assemble the center square of the tree block; add green border strips. Make 18 Santa blocks and 17 tree blocks.

Stitch French knots for Santas' eyes using three strands of floss.

ASSEMBLY: Starting with a Santa block in the upper left corner, alternate Santa and tree blocks. Assemble seven horizontal rows of five blocks each; sew the rows together.

Sew the 1½x37-inch red border strips to the top and bottom edges. Trim excess length; add the 1½x50-inch side borders. Sew the 4x46-inch tan print border strips to top and bottom edges; add the 4x60-inch tan print borders to sides.

MARKING AND QUILTING: Mark desired quilting design.

Layer quilt backing, batting, and top. Baste all layers together. Quilt as desired on marked lines. When quilting is complete, remove basting; trim batting and backing even with top.

BINDING: Sew the five binding strips together end to end. With wrong sides of fabric facing, fold strip in half lengthwise. Starting in the center of any side, match raw edges of binding and quilt. Sew around all sides, folding corners as you go. Overlap approximately ½ inch of binding at the starting point. Fold binding over raw edge; hand-sew to back.

Christmas Tree Advent Calendar

Shown on page 21.

The finished calendar measures 21¼x24¾ inches.

MATERIALS
¾ yard light print fabric for background
¾ yard green print fabric for tree
¼ yard fabric for binding
⅛ yard *each* of four coordinating print fabrics (we used dark rose, light rose, light green, and a pink, green and blue piece)
Scrap of brown fabric for tree trunk
Scrap of gold lamé for star
1 yard flannel fleecing
½ yard fusible webbing
24 ceramic novelty buttons
24 metal snaps
Tube of gold glitter puffy paint
¾-inch commercial number stencils
7 yards *each* of ¹/₁₆-inch-wide light and dark rose-colored ribbon
Matching threads; fiberfill

INSTRUCTIONS
Note: All strip cutting measurements include ¼-inch seam allowances. Add ¼-inch seam allowance to patterns, *opposite*

and on page 30. Sew all seams with right sides facing unless otherwise specified.

CUTTING: Trace the five tier patterns, *opposite* and on page 30, onto tracing paper; cut out. Fold tree fabric lengthwise. Pin five tier patterns along fabric fold; cut out. Repeat for facing pieces.

From the background fabric, cut one 18x23¼-inch rectangle. Cut two 2¼x8½-inch strips for the pieces that fit next to the trunk. Cut four 2¼-inch corner squares.

From the brown fabric, cut one 2¼x2-inch trunk.

Note: The packages along the sides of the calendar are made from the four coordinating fabrics. From each fabric, make six packages as directed *below* and arrange them randomly to make the side strips.

For the packages, make a 2¼-inch square cardboard template. Cut 18 squares from *each* of the four fabrics. (It takes three squares to make each package and lid.)

Cut 24 squares from the flannel fleecing for interfacing the package lids and one fleece piece for each tree tier.

From the binding fabric, cut two 2x45-inch strips.

Trace star pattern, *opposite*, onto tracing paper; cut out. Trace star pattern onto wrong side of gold fabric. Add a ³/₁₆-inch seam allowance before cutting the star from the fabric.

BACKGROUND ASSEMBLY: Sew the 2¼x8½-inch rectangles to the 2¼-inch sides of the trunk. Sew this strip to one 18-inch side of the background rectangle.

To make package strips that border the sides of the background, begin by first assembling the package lids (flaps). To make one lid, sew two matching squares together with a square of fleece on top. Sew around three sides. Turn, press, and machine-quilt a 1-inch square inside lid.

continued

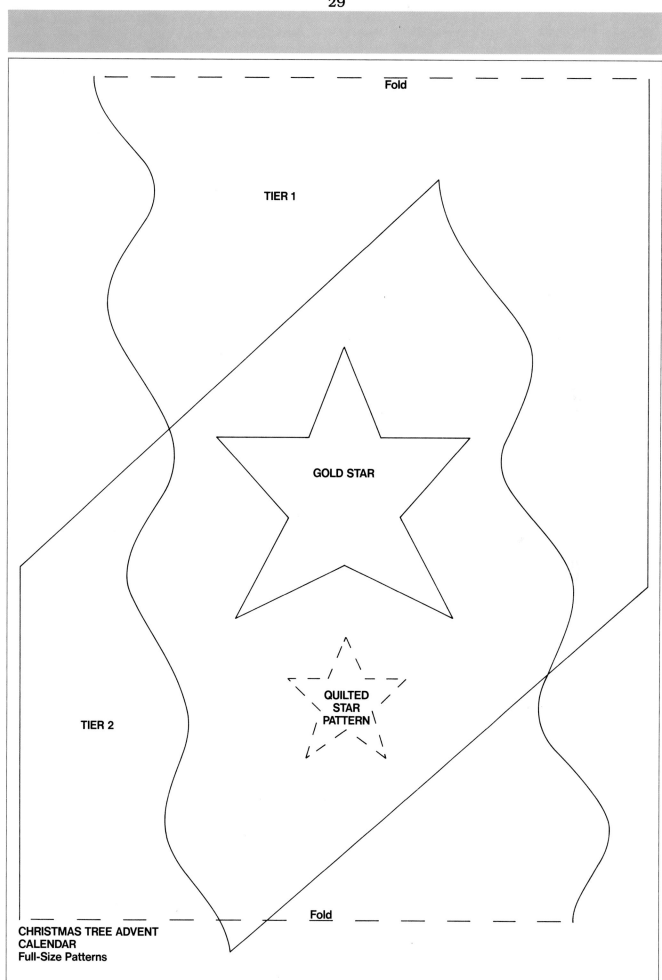

Fold

TIER 1

GOLD STAR

QUILTED
STAR
PATTERN

TIER 2

Fold

CHRISTMAS TREE ADVENT
CALENDAR
Full-Size Patterns

THE NIGHT BEFORE CHRISTMAS

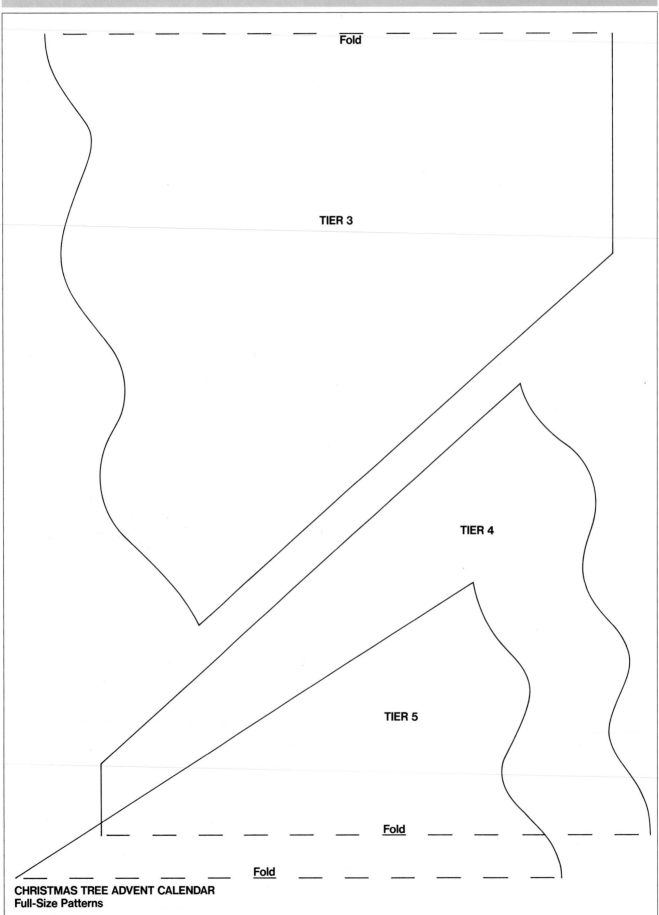

Fold

TIER 3

TIER 4

TIER 5

Fold

Fold

CHRISTMAS TREE ADVENT CALENDAR
Full-Size Patterns

Sew lids to one side of matching fabric squares to complete the 24 packages.

Keeping flaps free and ensuring they go in the same direction, sew 12 packages together to make one long strip. Make a second strip of the same length. Sew a corner background square to the top and bottom of each strip.

Sew the two package strips to opposite sides of the background rectangle.

BACKGROUND QUILTING: Layer the backing, batting, and top; baste layers together. Machine- or hand-quilt wavy lines across the background area. Quilt a star, using the dashed star pattern on page 29, in each background corner square. Quilt the tree trunk as desired. Remove basting.

BINDING: Sew the two 2x45-inch strips together to make a 90-inch-long binding strip. Fold strip in half lengthwise, wrong sides together. Sew binding to the top of the rectangle. Turn binding to back side and carefully hand-sew in place.

TREE ASSEMBLY: Following the manufacturer's instructions, fuse webbing to the wrong sides of the five separate tree tiers.

Begin with the top tier and layer the top (webbing side down), the matching tier facing (right side down), and then fleecing. Sew around all sides; trim seams and clip curves. Slit the back facing, turn tier inside out, and sew slit closed.

Assemble the remaining four tiers in a similar manner. For each tier, layer the three pieces. Sew the two sides and bottom edges together, leaving the top open. Clip the seams and turn each tier inside out. Baste the top edges together. Topstitch along the bottom edge of all five tiers.

Cut ribbon into twenty-four 8-inch pieces—12 of each color. Randomly tack each ribbon center to the five tiers. Tie the ends into a bow.

Beginning with the bottom tier, sew the sides of the tiers to the

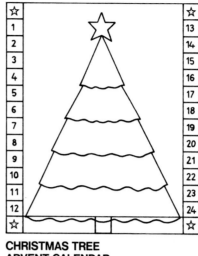

**CHRISTMAS TREE
ADVENT CALENDAR**

background fabric. Curve each piece out slightly from the backing. Refer to the diagram, *above,* for approximate placement. Tack the top raw edges to the background fabric to hold in place; leave the bottom rippled edge free.

FINISHING: Appliqué the gold star to the tree top. Hand-quilt around the star.

Use a pencil and the stencils to lightly trace the numbers 1–12 on the doors down the left side of the hanging, and 13–24 on the doors down the right side of the hanging. Go over the lines with the glitter paint; allow to dry.

Lightly mark 1¾-inch rays coming out from the star points. Go over these lines with the glitter paint. Allow to dry.

Cut ribbon into twenty-four 8-inch pieces; make 24 bows, and sew them securely to the top of each lid.

Cut twenty-four 4-inch pieces of ribbon. Sew them at the top (under the flap) of the inside of each package. Tie the buttons behind the flaps.

Matching snap pieces, center and sew a snap to the inside of each lid along the bottom edge and to the lower edge of each package.

Stuff a small amount of fiberfill behind each tree tier to add greater dimension.

The Night Before Christmas Afghan

Shown on pages 22 and 23.

Finished size is 46x58 inches.

MATERIALS
Brunswick Germantown Knitting Worsted (100-gram skeins): 8 skeins copen blue (4121) and 4 skeins ecru (4000)
Size 8 circular 36-inch knitting needles, or size to obtain gauge given
Size G crochet hook
Tapestry needle

Abbreviations: See page 15.
Gauge: 4¾ sts = 1 inch in pattern; 5¼ rows = 1 inch.

INSTRUCTIONS
Note: When changing yarn colors, always drop the color in use to the back side of the work. Bring the new color from underneath to twist the yarns and prevent holes. Catch the yarn you are carrying every 3 to 4 sts.

AFGHAN: For ease in working, if desired, photocopy the four charts on pages 32–35. Tape them together, lining up the center repeat rows that are shaded in gray. These shaded rows are for positioning; do not work these sts.

With copen blue, cast on 221 sts; do not join.

Working in st st, begin following chart at Row 2 (the cast on is Row 1). The squares with a symbol in them are ecru and the blank squares are copen blue. Complete the chart. Bind off.

FINISHING: With Size G crochet hook, sc evenly spaced around all sides of afghan, working 3 sc in each corner; join with sl st to first sc. Ch 1, do not turn. Working from left to right (reverse sc), sc in each sc around; fasten off. Weave in ends. Block right side of afghan on a well-padded surface.

THE NIGHT BEFORE CHRISTMAS AFGHAN

1 Square = 1 Stitch

THE NIGHT BEFORE CHRISTMAS

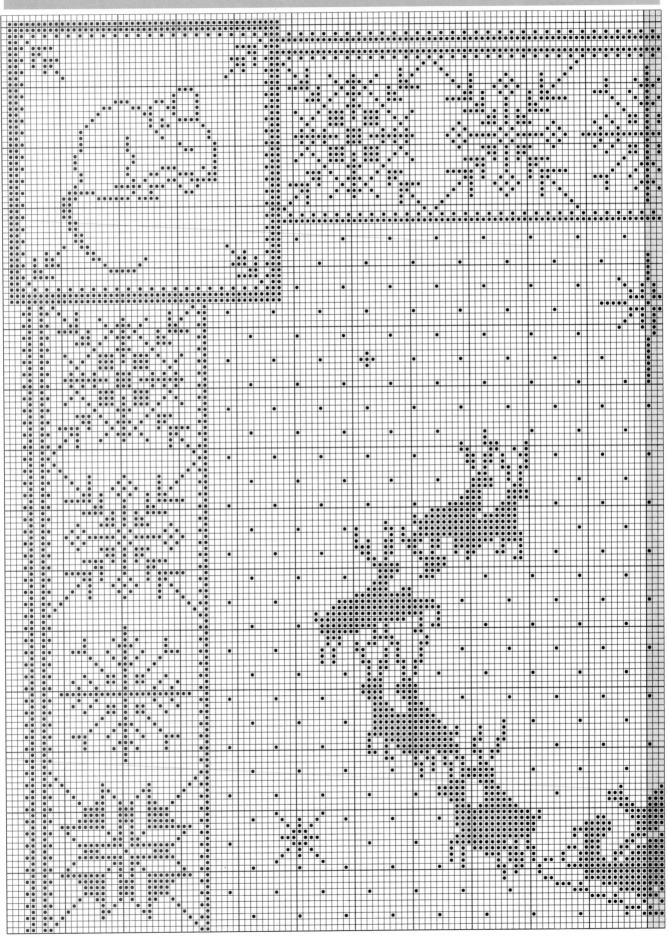

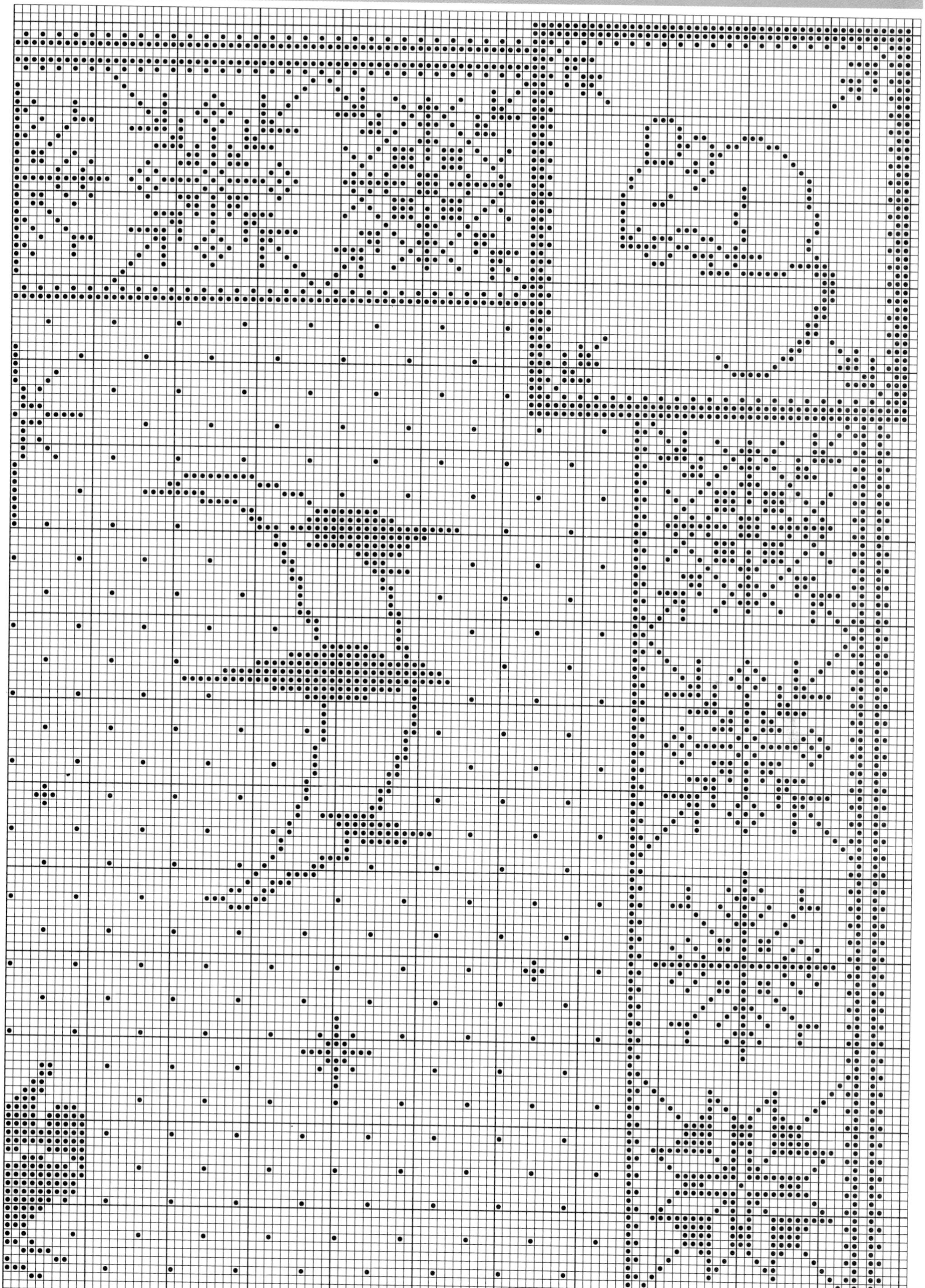

STAR DAZZLERS

TO BRIGHTEN THE SEASON

Shining symbol of the season, the star adds a special brilliance to any holiday project. To help you set your house aglow with Christmas spirit, we've selected nearly a dozen dazzling designs for you to knit, crochet, or quilt. Whatever your needlework preference, you're sure to find something splendid to brighten your home this season and for many years.

With stars brightly shining around a simple manger scene, the peaceable kingdom wall hanging, *right,* celebrates the Christmas story in a new and delightful way. Unlike most Nativities, this one is made to be mounted on a wall or hung above a mantel.

This enchanting appliquéd and quilted crèche is machine-satin-stitched with sprightly colored solid and pindotted fabrics. Work the center manger scene first. Then stitch the star and checkerboard background. With the addition of the red pindotted binding, the wall hanging measures 24x36 inches.

For the quartet of peaceable kingdom companion pillows, choose fabrics with a subtle pattern. Appliqué all pattern pieces to a muslin square and machine-satin-stitch the design outlines. Stitch pillow fronts to backing fabric and stuff with fiberfill.

Complete instructions and full-size patterns for these and all projects in this chapter begin on page 42.

A band of blazing stars accents the Christmas stocking and afghan, *above* and *opposite*. Worked with worsted-weight yarn in jewel-tone colors, this pair of star-patterned projects will make your home glow with the holiday spirit.

Following a charted design, the afghan is knit in rounds and cut apart when completed. An easy knitted border is added to each long side. The stocking instructions include an alphabet chart so you can personalize the stocking with the name of your choice.

STAR DAZZLERS

Stitch a spectacular skirt to circle your tree year after year. The quilted tree skirt, *left,* features pieced stars and appliquéd holly leaves. This skirt also doubles as a table covering at holiday time.

To complement the tree skirt, make the simple stitch-and-stuff star and holly leaf ornaments, *left.* Small red buttons become the holly berries at the top of each leaf.

A dazzling star motif is the focus of the glorious granny afghan, *above.* This 40x55-inch throw is crocheted by the square in four brilliant colors and edged with a wide picot and scallop border.

Peaceable Kingdom Wall Hanging

Shown on pages 36 and 37.

Wall hanging measures 24x36 inches.

MATERIALS
⅝ yard *each* of royal blue, green, and yellow fabrics
½ yard red pindotted fabric
¼ yard *or* 12x8-inch piece *each* of pindotted fabrics for appliqués in off-white, gray, burnt orange, tan, and brown
32x40-inch quilt batting
½ yard of fusible webbing
2 spools of yellow thread
1 spool *each* of red and royal blue thread
32x40-inch fabric for backing and hanging sleeve
Plastic or cardboard for templates; ruler
Tracing paper and pencil
Rotary cutter and mat (optional)

INSTRUCTIONS
CUTTING: From both the royal blue and green fabrics, cut four 2½-inch-wide strips across the width of the fabric. Cut one strip of *each* color into thirds, approximately 2½x14 inches. Set all the strips aside for the checkerboard. From the remaining fabric, cut an 8¾x20½-inch blue piece and a 5¾x20½-inch green piece for the center rectangle.

From the red dot fabric, cut two strips 2½x29 inches and two strips 2½x41 inches for the binding. For the inner border, cut two strips 1½x23 inches and two strips 1½x8½ inches. Save the scraps of red dot fabric for the cow appliqués.

Trace the full-size appliqué patterns, *right* and *opposite*. Make a template for each shape, completing patterns shown on the fold. Use the Star 1 template to mark and cut 66 stars from the yellow fabric.

Mark the remaining templates on the right sides of the appropri-

ate appliqué fabrics, reversing one pattern of each animal. Attach fusible webbing to the wrong sides of the marked appliqué shapes following manufacturer's instructions. Cut out shapes.

STITCHING THE CENTER APPLIQUÉ: With right sides facing, sew the blue and green 20½-inch-long pieces together along one long side using ¼-inch seams to make the center background; press seam open. Following the diagram, *opposite*, fuse appliqué pieces to the background. The portion where dashed lines appear on the pattern falls behind the overlapping shape. First fuse all pieces that are partially covered by another piece first.

continued

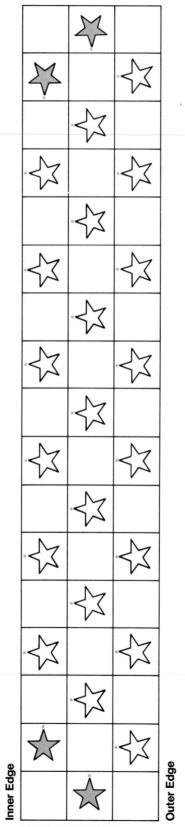

PANEL A DIAGRAM

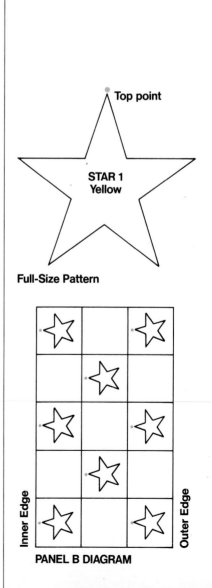

Top point

STAR 1
Yellow

Full-Size Pattern

PANEL B DIAGRAM

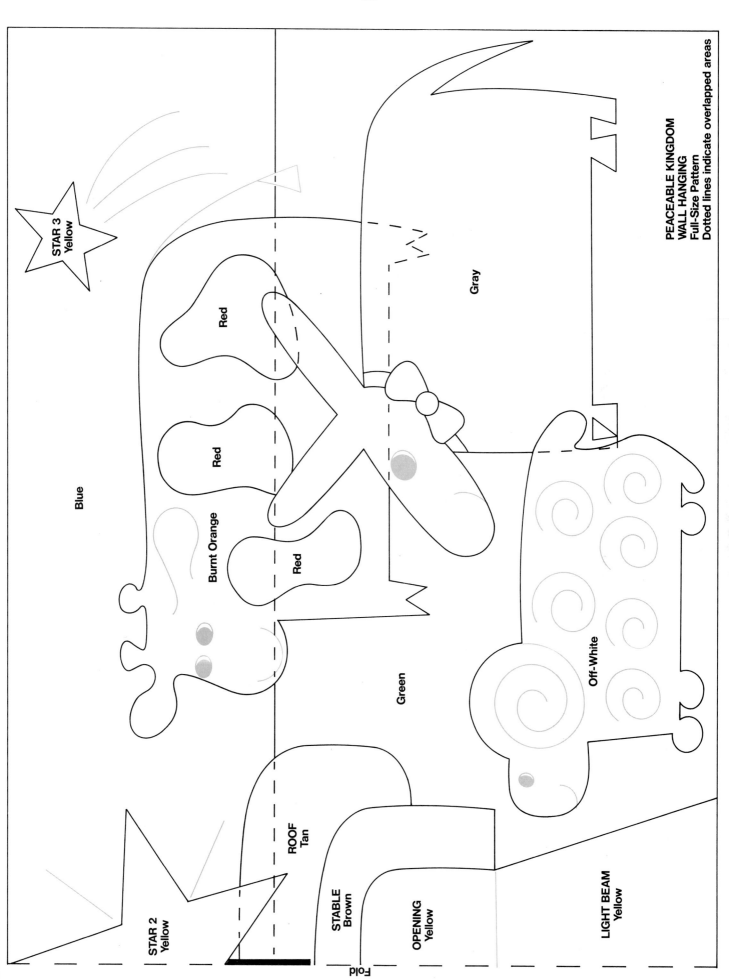

STAR 3
Yellow

Red

Red

Blue

Burnt Orange

Red

Gray

Green

Off-White

STAR 2
Yellow

ROOF
Tan

Fold

STABLE
Brown

OPENING
Yellow

LIGHT BEAM
Yellow

PEACEABLE KINGDOM
WALL HANGING
Full-Size Pattern
Dotted lines indicate overlapped areas

Adjust the stitch to a narrow, tight zigzag. Using royal blue thread, stitch features on all animals as indicated by the blue lines on patterns. Appliqué the cows' red spots and the green bows on each donkey using the same stitch width.

PIECING BORDER SQUARES: Sew one long 2½-inch-wide blue strip to each side of one long matching green strip. Make a second strip set with the remaining blue strip and two green strips. Use the short strips to make matching strip sets. Press all seams toward the green fabric.

Measure and cut 2½-inch segments down the length of each strip set. Cut 22 segments from *each* color combination.

Refer to the diagrams for Panel A and Panel B on page 42 and sew together the correct number of segments for each panel. Panel A has green squares in each corner; Panel B has blue corners. Make two of each panel. Press.

Center a yellow star on each blue square, aligning the top point of each star toward the inner edge of the panel; baste into place. *Note:* The dot placed above the *top point* of the stars will help you locate their positions on the panels. The stars marked in gray on the diagram of Panel A are facing in rather than facing up (notice the way the *top point* is always pointing toward the center motifs in the photograph on pages 36 and 37). Turn these stars one-quarter turn to the right so they are pointing toward the center motif. This arrangement is necessary for turning the corners of the checkerboard star pattern.

With yellow thread, machine-appliqué each star onto the blue background squares.

ASSEMBLY: Sew a 1½x8½-inch red strip to each short side of the center block. Next, sew one 1½x23-inch red strip to each long side.

Once the center block is bordered in red, sew a Panel B to each short side, making sure the stars point in toward the center block.

Next, sew one Panel A to each long side, making sure all seam lines meet neatly at the corners and that the top points of the stars face in toward the center block. Press.

FINISHING: Cut a 4x35-inch strip from the backing fabric; set aside for the hanging sleeve. Lay the remaining backing fabric right side down, with the batting on top. Center the pieced quilt on the batting; baste together.

Using yellow thread, zigzag-stitch the stars, light beam, and stable opening. Use the narrow zigzag setting to stitch rays coming from the stars.

Use blue thread to zigzag-stitch the animals, the remaining parts of the stable, and the roof. Zigzag along the seam where the green background meets the blue sky.

Hand- or machine-embroider each cow's tail.

Using blue thread, hand- or machine-quilt "in the ditch" along all seams of the checkerboard or as desired. Trim excess batting and backing even with the quilt top.

Sew the 2½x29-inch red binding strips to the quilt sides, then attach the two remaining red strips to the long sides. Fold the red edge over, toward the back of the quilt, making a 1-inch border. Turn under the raw edges and hand-sew to the backing. Remove all basting stitches. Press lightly.

Turn under and topstitch a ¼-inch hem on all edges of the sleeve fabric. Center sleeve at the top of the hanging just below the red border fabric. Hand-sew the long edges to the backing, taking care not to come through to the front. Press. Pass a dowel rod through the opening to hang.

Peaceable Kingdom Pillows

Shown on pages 36 and 37.

Pillows measure approximately 8½x12 inches.

MATERIALS

½ yard fabric for *each* of the following fabrics: yellow for star, brown print for cow, gray print for donkey, and cream print for sheep
8x6-inch scrap of contrasting fabric for cow's spots
15-inch square *each* of muslin and fleece for each pillow
48 inches of narrow cording for piping on each pillow
Paper-backed fusible webbing
Bright colored threads
Polyester fiberfill
Nonpermanent fabric marker
Typing paper for embroidery
Brown and black embroidery floss
Graph paper
Large-eyed tapestry needle

INSTRUCTIONS

Cut and set aside two 9-inch squares of *each* yellow star or animal print fabric for *each* pillow back.

Enlarge pattern shapes, *opposite*, onto graph paper. Trace shapes and details onto the right sides of the remaining yellow star and animal print fabrics.

Following the manufacturer's instructions, fuse webbing to the wrong sides of animal print fabrics and yellow star fabric. Cut out shapes; center and fuse each to a muslin square. Cut out and fuse contrasting spots to cow. Machine-satin-stitch around each shape. Use typing paper under the muslin when stitching to help avoid stretching the material. Pull threads to wrong side; knot ends.

Use a narrower satin stitch to outline the mouths and the sheep's curls.

With three strands of black floss, outline-stitch the circles around the eyes. Fill in the pupils with satin stitches.

Use the fabric marker to draw a sewing line on the muslin around the appliqués, ½ inch outside the design, simplifying the shape around details. Do not cut out the shapes.

To make piping, use narrow bias strips of matching appliqué

PEACEABLE KINGDOM PILLOWS

1 Square = 1 Inch

fabric to cover cording. Back muslin with fleece and baste piping to pillow top on drawn sewing line, sewing through all layers.

Sew two 9-inch pieces of matching backing fabric together along one side to make the center back seam, leaving a 3-inch opening at the center for turning. With right sides facing, sew back to front on piping line. Trim excess muslin and backing, cutting the seam allowance to ¼ inch. Clip curves. Turn and stuff. Slip-stitch the opening closed.

For the cow's tail, cut six 6-ply lengths of brown floss, *each* 10 inches long. Thread the needle with all lengths; bring the needle through the fabric at the back end of the cow at the X mark on the pattern. Remove needle; pull floss through. Separate floss into three equal sections and braid up to 4 inches. Tie off tail end with a scrap of floss; trim.

Star Snowflake Afghan

Shown on pages 38 and 39.

Afghan measures 44x54 inches.

MATERIALS
Lane Borgosesia Knitaly (100-gram skein): 3 skeins red (3793), 3 skeins white, and 11 skeins green (1360)
Size 8 circular 36-inch knitting needle or size to obtain gauge
Size 7 circular 36-inch knitting needle, for picking up stitches
Size H crochet hook
Tapestry needle

Abbreviations: See page 15.
Gauge: 5 sts = 1 inch; 7 rows = 1 inch on Size 8 needles.

INSTRUCTIONS
Using Size 8 needle and white yarn, cast on 224 sts; place marker; join, taking care not to twist sts. P 2 rnds.

Note: When working from the chart on page 46, always begin at the lower right corner. Afghan now begins to work in rnds. K all rnds unless stated otherwise, except always p the last 3 sts of each rnd. These p sts form the cutting ridge when the knitting is completed, and are not included in the chart.

Rnds 1 and 2: K with white.
Rnd 3: K with green.
Rnd 4: K with white.
Rnd 5: Rep Rnd 3.
Rnd 6: Rep Rnd 4.

continued

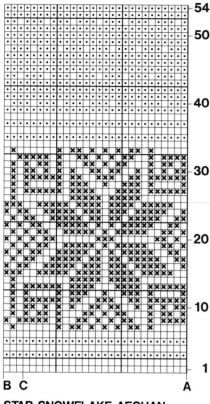

B C   **A**

STAR SNOWFLAKE AFGHAN

COLOR KEY
- ⊡ **Green**
- ⊠ **Red**

1 Square = 1 Stitch

Rnd 7: Referring to the chart, *above,* work from A–B seven times, then work from A–C one time more.

Continue following the chart through Rnd 54. Rep rnds 39–54 until afghan measures 6 inches less than desired length for approximately 50 inches. End after completing Rnd 53. Repeat rnds 2–37. End red and green yarns. K 2 rnds. P 2 rnds. Bind off loosely.

Turn tube inside out; weave in ends.

EDGE BANDS: Carefully block the 3-purl stitch cutting ridge. With sewing machine and overcast or zigzag stitch, stitch along one side of the purled ridge, stitching closely to the first stitch of the main body of the afghan. Stitch the full length of the afghan. Stitch again over the first row of stitching. Repeat the stitching twice on the other side of the purl ridge. Carefully cut between the two rows of machine stitching to open the afghan.

To determine the number of stitches to pick up along the edges, you need to measure the length of your afghan and multiply it by your stitch gauge. For example, if your afghan measures 56 inches and your stitch gauge is 5 stitches to the inch, then you will pick up and knit 280 stitches along each of the edges.

To make sure your stitches are evenly distributed along the length, use straight pins to divide the edge into four even sections. As you begin to pick up the stitches with the Size 7 needle, you'll want, for example, to have 70 stitches in each section if you are picking up 280 stitches.

Row 1 (wrong side): With green and Size 8 needle, k across.

Row 2 (right side): K across.

Row 3: P across.

Rep rows 2 and 3 three times more; bind off.

With green yarn, sew the bind-off edge to the back side of the afghan along the white pick-up row.

Work the band on the opposite edge of the afghan.

FRINGE: Cut 12-inch lengths of yarn. Use red or white strands with green to add color or use all green. Holding two folded strands together, use the crochet hook to pull the strands through the first st along the cast on edge; pull ends through loop just formed. Add fringe in every other st across the cast-on and bind-off edges. Block fringe and afghan. Trim fringe ends even.

Star Snowflake Stocking

Shown on pages 38 and 39.

Finished stocking measures 23 inches long.

MATERIALS

Lane Borgosesia Knitaly (100-gram skeins): 1 skein *each* of red (3793), green (1360), and white

Size 7 double-pointed knitting needles or size to obtain gauge given below

Size 7 circular 16-inch knitting needle or size to obtain gauge given below

Stitch marker; tapestry needle

Scrap yarn the same weight in a contrasting color

Abbreviations: See page 15.

Gauge: 5 sts = 1 inch; 7 rows = 1 inch.

INSTRUCTIONS

With white, cast on 82 sts onto circular needle. Place marker and join, taking care not to twist sts.

Rnd 1: P.

Rnd 2: K.

Rnds 3–37: Following Chart 1, *opposite,* k working between A and B twice. Always begin each rnd at A. At end of Rnd 37, fasten off red and green yarns.

Rnds 38 and 39: With white p.

Rnds 40–47: K.

Rnds 48 and 49: P.

Rnd 50: Drop white yarn to back of work, with red k around and dec 2 sts evenly spaced—80 sts.

Rnd 51: With red k.

Rnds 52–59: Working from Chart 2, *opposite,* rep between A–B around. Rep Chart 2 four times more; then rep the first seven rows of chart. Fasten off white.

SETTING UP THE HEEL: *Note:* These instructions create the placement for the heel that will be inserted later.

Sl last 20 sts worked back onto

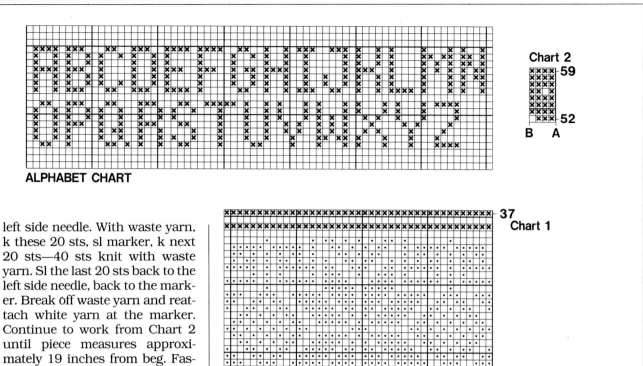

ALPHABET CHART

Chart 2

59

52

B A

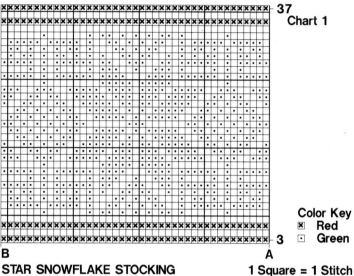

37

Chart 1

Color Key
⊠ Red
⊡ Green

STAR SNOWFLAKE STOCKING

1 Square = 1 Stitch

B   A

left side needle. With waste yarn, k these 20 sts, sl marker, k next 20 sts—40 sts knit with waste yarn. Sl the last 20 sts back to the left side needle, back to the marker. Break off waste yarn and reattach white yarn at the marker. Continue to work from Chart 2 until piece measures approximately 19 inches from beg. Fasten off red and white yarns. Attach green.

TOE: *Rnd 1:* K. Change to dpn and set up needles as follows:

Rnd 2: First needle, k 20 sts; second needle, k 40 sts; third needle, k last 20 sts.

Rnd 3: K to last 3 sts on first needle, k 2 tog, k 1; on second needle, sl 1, k 1, psso, k to last 3 sts, k 2 tog, k 1; on third needle, sl 1, k 1, psso, k to end.

Rnd 4: K even.

Rep rnds 3 and 4 until first and third needles contain 7 sts each, and second needle contains 14 sts—28 sts. Fasten off leaving a 15-inch tail. Using a tapestry needle graft sts from first and third needles to the sts on the second needle with the Kitchener stitch. Weave in ends. Block lightly.

HEEL: Carefully remove waste yarn. Divide and sl 40 sts above heel opening to first and second needle—20 sts on each needle. Sl 40 sts below heel opening to third needle. Join green yarn at beg of first needle.

Rnd 1: K.

Rnd 2: K 1, sl 1, k 1, psso, k to last 3 sts of second needle, k 2 tog, k 1; on third needle k 1, sl 1, k 1, psso, k to last 3 sts, k 2 tog, k 1.

Rnd 3: K.

Rep rnds 2 and 3 until first and second needles contain 9 sts each, and 18 sts remain on the third needle. Fasten off leaving a 15-inch tail. Using a tapestry needle graft sts from first and second needles to the sts on the third needle with the Kitchener stitch. Weave in ends.

NAME BAND: Use the Alphabet Chart, *top left,* to duplicate-stitch the name onto the white band at the top of the stocking. Refer to the duplicate-stitch diagram on page 14. Block into stocking shape.

Star Tree Skirt

Shown on pages 40 and 41.

Tree skirt measures 51 inches in diameter.

MATERIALS

1½ yards green print fabric for patchwork and binding
1 yard muslin
⅝ yard *each* red and dark green fabrics for star
⅜ yard green print fabric for holly leaves
¼ yard gold print fabric
¼ yard red print fabric
3 yards *each* batting and backing fabric
Quilting thread and needle
Template plastic; 6 metal snaps
Pencil; ruler
Rotary cutter and mat (optional)
Artist's right-angle triangle

continued

STAR DAZZLERS

STAR TREE SKIRT DIAGRAM

INSTRUCTIONS

Note: All seams are ¼ inch wide and sewn with fabrics' right sides together, unless otherwise noted.

CUTTING: Trace the two diamond patterns on page 50 onto template plastic. Mark grain lines; cut shapes from plastic.

Cut red and dark green star fabrics into five 3⅛-inch-wide strips across the fabric width. Use the larger diamond template to mark

six or seven diamonds on each strip, with the grain line horizontal. Cut out 32 diamonds from each fabric.

Cut a 23½-inch square from the green patchwork fabric. Cut this into four 11¾-inch squares, then cut each square into quarters diagonally to make a total of 16 triangles. Set these triangles aside for the outer edge. Cut two green strips 2¾x42 inches; from these, cut thirty 2¾-inch squares.

Cut each of these in quarters diagonally to make 36 triangles. If you have cut this fabric correctly, you should have plenty left for bias binding.

From the muslin, cut a 23-inch length. With a pencil and ruler, mark one side with four 5¾-inch-wide strips. Use the triangle to mark a 45-degree angle at the beginning of each strip. Measure and mark four increments of 8⅜ inches along both top and bottom lines of each strip, starting at the marked angle. Connecting the marks should delineate large diamonds with a horizontal grain line. Cut 16 large diamonds.

Use the small diamond template to mark and cut 32 diamonds *each* from the gold print and remaining muslin fabrics.

For the holly appliqué, trace 32 leaves onto the right side of the leaf fabric. Add a $^3/_{16}$-inch seam allowance around each tracing to cut on. Cut forty-eight 2-inch-diameter circles from the red print fabric for berries.

LARGE CENTER STAR: Assemble the 64 red and green diamonds into 32 seamed pairs. Matching center seam lines, join two pairs to make one large diamond. Make 16 large diamonds. Press the seams toward the darker fabric.

Use eight large diamonds for the center star. Join diamonds into four star quarters, then join the quarters to make two half stars. Match seams carefully.

Join the halves to make one full star. Sew the center seam from one end to the middle, leaving the rest of the center seam open.

SMALL STAR BLOCKS: Assemble four gold and four muslin diamonds into an eight-pointed star as shown in the photograph on page 40. Set in squares and triangles to complete the block. Make seven *complete* small star blocks.

The eighth star is split by the skirt opening. For this star, make two star halves, setting in squares and triangles to complete the triangular units.

APPLIQUÉ: Center two holly leaves vertically on each large muslin diamond. Appliqué leaves in place.

To make a berry, stitch a loose basting stitch all around a red fabric circle, ¼ inch from the edge. Pull thread ends tightly to gather the circle into a small "yo-yo." Appliqué three berries at the center of each leaf pair.

ASSEMBLY AND QUILTING: Refer to tree skirt diagram, *opposite*, to assemble all units. Be sure to leave the center seam open at the back of the skirt.

Cut and piece batting and backing as necessary to make a 54-inch square. Leave the back center seam open. Sandwich batting between quilt top and backing; baste layers together. Quilt or tie the tree skirt as desired. When quilting is complete, trim batting and backing even with tree skirt.

BINDING: Measure the center seam opening—it should be approximately 26 inches long. From green print binding fabric, cut two 4-inch-wide strips that measure the length of the opening plus ½ inch (26½ inches).

Fold each strip in half lengthwise. Stitch across one short end; turn corners right side out and press. Match one strip to left side of opening, right sides together, with the finished corner of the binding positioned at the center of the tree skirt. Stitch through all layers, sewing from the center to the outside edge of the skirt. Fold binding strip over raw edge and hand-sew onto backing. Repeat with remaining strip on right side of opening. At center, tack the two binding strips together where they meet.

From the remaining green print binding fabric, cut approximately 180 inches of 1¾-inch-wide continuous bias binding. (See page 25 for instructions.) Press binding strip in half lengthwise, wrong sides together.

Starting at one side of the back opening, match raw edges and right sides of binding and quilt top. Leave ½ inch of binding extending past the opening edge. Machine-stitch ¼ inch from the edge all around the tree skirt. Cut away excess length of binding, leaving ½ inch extra beyond the opening. Turn binding over the raw edge; hand-sew to backing. Turn in ends at openings.

Remove basting. Evenly space and sew six snaps inside the opening.

Holly and Star Ornaments

Shown on pages 40 and 41.

Ornaments measure 4¾ inches long.

MATERIALS
For one ornament
Scraps of cream and gold or other holiday fabrics
Fleece
Thread in matching or contrasting colors
Polyester fiberfill
Tracing paper
Typing paper
Fusible webbing paper
Three round red buttons for the holly berries

INSTRUCTIONS
For one holly ornament
Trace the holly leaf pattern on page 50 onto fusible webbing paper. Following the manufacturer's directions, fuse the webbing to the wrong side of the fabric. Retrace the leaf shape and add the vein details (marked in blue on the pattern) onto the right side of the fabric. Remove the paper. Fuse the fabric to a layer of fleece.

With green thread and typing paper against the fleece side, machine-satin-stitch the leaf vein. Remove the typing paper.

With wrong sides facing, machine-stitch the leaf front to another scrap of matching fabric. Cut out the leaf just beyond the stitching. Machine-satin-stitch around the outside edge.

Make a slit in backing fabric; stuff with fiberfill. Sew slit closed. Sew buttons to top of each leaf.

continued

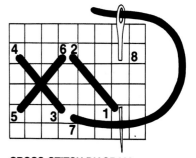

CROSS-STITCH DIAGRAM

STAR DAZZLERS

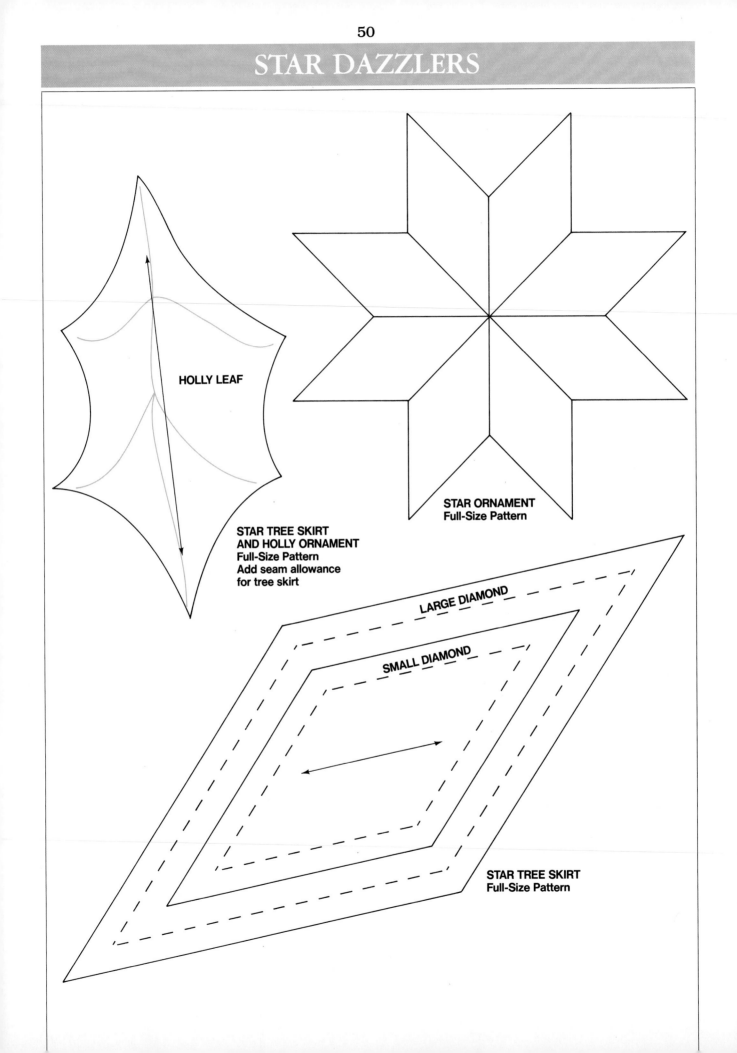

HOLLY LEAF

STAR TREE SKIRT
AND HOLLY ORNAMENT
Full-Size Pattern
Add seam allowance
for tree skirt

STAR ORNAMENT
Full-Size Pattern

LARGE DIAMOND

SMALL DIAMOND

STAR TREE SKIRT
Full-Size Pattern

For one star ornament

Trace star shape and inner lines, *opposite,* onto fusible webbing paper. Fuse webbing to the wrong side of the cream-colored fabric. Trace star shape and inner lines (for diamonds) onto the right side of the fabric. Remove the paper and fuse to a layer of fleece.

Trace the four diamond shapes onto fusible webbing paper and fuse to the wrong side of the gold fabric. Cut out four gold diamonds for *each* ornament and fuse them to the right side of the cream-colored star shape, alternating the gold and cream-colored diamonds.

With typing paper against the fleece side of the star, machine-satin-stitch the inside lines of the diamonds using either red, green, or blue thread.

Using the same color of thread and with wrong sides facing, machine-stitch the star to the matching cream-colored backing fabric going completely around the star shape. Cut out the star just beyond the stitching. Machine-satin-stitch around the outside edge.

Make a small slit in the backing fabric; stuff with fiberfill. Whipstitch the slit closed.

Granny Square Star Afghan

Shown on page 41.

Afghan measures 40x55 inches.

MATERIALS

Caron Dawn Sayelle knitting worsted (3.5-ounce skein): 2 skeins scarlet (0326), 3 skeins sun gold (0358), 3 skeins mulberry (0324), and 5 skeins jade (0307)
Size H crochet hook
Tapestry needle

Abbreviations: See page 15.
Gauge: One motif measures 7¼ inches square.

INSTRUCTIONS
STAR MOTIF

With scarlet, ch 3; join with sl st to form ring.

Rnd 1: Ch 1, * sc in ring, ch 4, sc in second ch from hook; sc in each of next 2 chs; rep from * 4 times more; join with sl st to sc at beg of rnd—5 spokes made. Fasten off scarlet.

Rnd 2: Join sun gold with sc in top st of any spoke; * in sc between spokes, work trc, dc, and trc; sc in top of next spoke; rep from * around; join with sl st to beg sc. Do not fasten off.

Rnd 3: * In next dc work hdc, dc, trc, ch 1, trc, dc, and hdc; sl st in sc at top of spoke; rep from * around; join with sl st to beg hdc; fasten off sun gold.

Rnd 4: Join jade in back lp of any ch-1 of the previous rnd with sl st; * in sl st at top of next spoke, work trc, 3 dc, and trc; sl st in back lp of next ch-1; rep from * around; join to beg sl st; fasten off jade.

Rnd 5: Join mulberry with sc in top of any dc; work 2 sc in *each* dc, trc, and sl st around motif—60 scs; join with sl st to beg sc; fasten off mulberry.

Rnd 6: (For this rnd work in back lps only.) With star point up, count to the left 8 scs, join scarlet with sl st; ch 6, trc in next sc; * dc in next sc, hdc in next 2 sc, sc in next 7 sc, hdc in next 2 sc, dc in next sc, trc in next sc, ch 2, trc in next sc; rep from * around; join with sl st in fourth ch of beg ch-6; fasten off scarlet.

Rnd 7: Join jade with sc in any ch-2 corner sp; ch 2, sc in same space; * sc in each of next 15 sts; in corner sp work sc, ch 2, and sc; rep from * around; join with sl st in first sc; do not fasten off.

Rnd 8: Sl st into corner sp, in same sp work sc, ch 2, and sc; Work as for Rnd 7, having 17 sts along sides and sc, ch 2, sc in each corner; join to first sc; fasten off jade.

Rnd 9: Join sun gold in any ch-2 corner sp; ch 2, in same sp work hdc, ch 3, and 2 hdc; * (sk next sc, 2 hdc in next sc) 9 times; sk next sc; in corner sp work 2 hdc, ch 3, and 2 hdc; rep from * around; join with sl st to top of ch-2 at beg of rnd; fasten off sun gold.

Rnd 10: Join mulberry in any ch-3 corner sp, ch 2, in same sp work hdc, ch 3, and 2 hdc; * sk 2 hdc, 2 hdc in sp bet next 2 dc-grps; rep from * around, working 2 hdc, ch 3, and 2 hdc in each ch-3 corner sp; join with sl st to top of beg ch-2; fasten off.

ASSEMBLY: Assemble the afghan by whipstitching the motifs together using mulberry yarn. Make five strips, *each* strip consisting of seven motifs. Whipstitch strips together, carefully matching the seams where the motifs are joined together.

BORDER: *Rnd 1:* With right side facing, join jade yarn with sc in any st; work sc evenly spaced around afghan working 3 sc in each corner st; join to first sc.

Rnd 2: Ch 3, work dc in each sc around; in center st of 3-sc corner grp, work 2 dc, ch 1, and 2 dc; join with sl st to top of beg ch-3.

Rnd 3: Ch 3, dc in each dc around; in ch-1 corner sp work 2 dc, ch 1, 2 dc; join to top of beg ch-3; fasten off.

Rnd 4: Join jade yarn with sl st in fourth dc to right of any ch-1 corner sp, sk 3 dc; **in ch-1 corner sp work 4 dc, ch 3, sl st into third ch from hook—picot made, and 4 dc; sk 3 dc, sl st into next dc—corner scallop made; sk 2 dc and work 4 dc into next dc, make picot, 4 dc; sk 3 dc, sl st into next dc—scallop made** * sk 2 dc; work scallop in next dc; sk 2 dc, sl st in next dc; rep from * to next corner. Follow directions for corner scallop and work as established for remaining 3 sides. Join to beg sl st; fasten off.

Weave in all ends and block the finished afghan.

A GARDEN OF POINSETTIAS

♦ ♦ ♦

The poinsettia, with its brilliant red blooms and shadowing green bracts, is the favorite flower of the Christmas season. It's no wonder holiday crafters long to preserve the beauty of this glorious blossom. Here you'll find poinsettia-patterned projects you can stitch now and enjoy year after year.

The legend of the poinsettia has its roots in Mexico where it's appropriately called the "Flower of Christmas Eve." The story tells about a little boy named Pablo who was anxious to visit the manger of his village church on Christmas Eve. Saddened because he had no lavish gifts to take, he gathered green branches from a poinsettia bush to lay at the foot of the manger. Other children laughed and made fun of him. But when they glanced a second time, brilliant red star-shaped flowers miraculously glowed from the tip of each branch.

Festive red and green fabrics glow against a snowy white background on our poinsettia quilt, *right*. A graceful arrangement of appliquéd flowers and greenery accents this old-time bed cover that's been lavishly quilted by hand and embellished with French knot flower centers.

Stitch this lovely 75x90-inch heritage quilt to share with holiday houseguests and family members for years to come.

Instructions for all projects in this chapter begin on page 56.

A garden of Christmas greenery patterns the 62x73-inch afghan, *opposite.* Crochet each background panel separately using worsted-weight yarn and the afghan-stitch technique. Then, cross-stitch the poinsettias and garlands of holly.

A lovely bunch of poinsettias bloom atop the 24x28-inch miniature quilt, *above.*

For the center rectangle, alternate the appliquéd blooms with hand-quilted squares. Borders of a striped Christmas print fabric complete this charming piece.

A GARDEN OF POINSETTIAS

Poinsettia Quilt

Shown on pages 52 and 53.

Finished quilt is approximately 75x90 inches.

MATERIALS

5½ yards of 90- or 108-inch-wide white cotton fabric for the quilt top and back
1½ yards of red fabric
1 yard of dark green fabric
½ yard of medium green
Red, medium green, and dark green embroidery floss
Tracing paper
Cardboard or plastic for templates
Quilt batting
Yardstick
Tailor's chalk pencil or water-erasable marking pen

INSTRUCTIONS

Trace and make cardboard or plastic templates for the full-size patterns, *opposite.* For the leaf patterns, make separate templates for the dark green and medium green sections. To make the stem pattern, trace the two stem sections, aligning the A–B marks on both sections to make one stem piece.

CUTTING INSTRUCTIONS: To mark and cut the appliqué pieces, draw around the template lightly with a pencil or tailor's chalk on the right side of the fabric, allowing approximately ½ inch between pieces. Cut out the appliqué pieces from fabrics, adding 3/16 inch for seam allowances.

From the red fabric, cut 256 poinsettia petals (eight for each flower).

From the medium green fabric, cut pieces for 28 large leaves and 32 small leaves.

From the dark green fabric, cut 28 stems. From the remaining fabric, cut pieces for 28 large leaves and 32 small leaves.

Divide the white fabric into two equal lengths and cut in half. Re-serve one length for the quilt back. Use the second length for the quilt top.

TO PREPARE THE PIECES: Fold the quilt top into fourths by folding it in half horizontally and then in half vertically; lightly press the fold lines to form creases. Using the crease lines as positioning guides, use the chalk pencil or water-erasable marker and yardstick to draw a 31x46½-inch rectangle in the center of the quilt. Measure 15½ inches from the center rectangle on all sides and draw a larger rectangle around the center rectangle. Mark the position for one poinsettia center at all corners of both rectangles. In addition, measure 15½-inch increments to mark placement for centers of remaining 20 flowers on both rectangles. At this point you have determined positions for 28 flowers. There are four additional flowers that will be marked and positioned later in the instructions.

Prepare the appliqué pieces by basting the seam allowances to the wrong side of the fabric along the outlines of the shapes. Do not baste under the side that runs down the leaf center on the medium green leaf sections; the dark green leaf sections will cover this edge.

TO APPLIQUÉ THE INNER RECTANGLE: Referring to the photo on pages 52 and 53, pin or baste the vine appliqué sections between the markings for flowers, centering the curves of the vine along the rectangular guidelines. Arrange the leaves following the pattern placement along the vines. Do not pin the extra four leaves to the quilt top at this time.

To form one poinsettia, position eight petals around the center mark, spacing the petals so there is an approximately 1¼-inch-diameter circular opening for the flower center.

Pin or baste pieces for a poinsettia at each center mark around the inner rectangle. Referring to the photo on pages 52 and 53, pin or baste the remaining four flowers to the inside of each corner flower and add the four extra small leaves along the outside edges of the vine to fill the space at each of the four corners.

When all pieces are in position, appliqué the pieces to the quilt top, using thread colors to match the appliqué shapes.

Using three strands of red, medium green, and dark green embroidery floss in random order, and referring to the diagram *below,* make French knots for the flower centers. Make knots to fill the centers of the flowers.

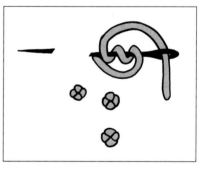

FRENCH KNOT DIAGRAM

TO APPLIQUÉ THE OUTSIDE RECTANGLE: Refer to the instructions for placing the pieces on the inner rectangle but do not add any additional flowers or leaves in the corners. Place a flower at each corner and every 15½ inches around the rectangle with a section of vine and two leaves between the flowers. When all pieces are in postion, appliqué them in place and embroider the flower centers.

continued

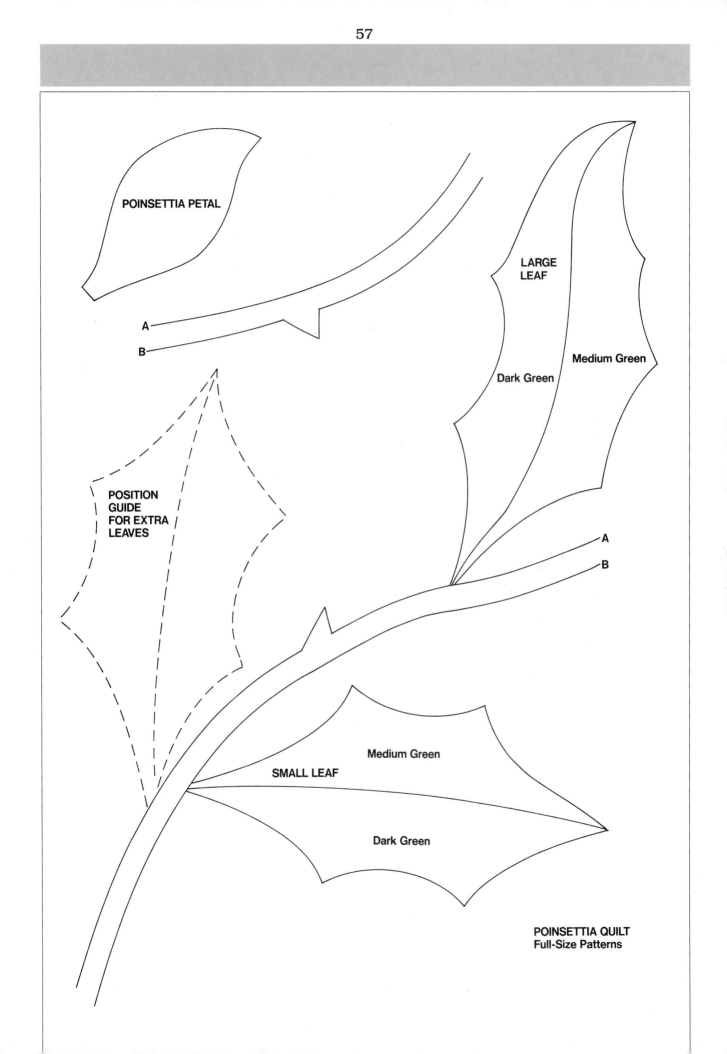

POINSETTIA PETAL

LARGE LEAF

Dark Green

Medium Green

A
B

POSITION GUIDE FOR EXTRA LEAVES

A
B

Medium Green

SMALL LEAF

Dark Green

POINSETTIA QUILT
Full-Size Patterns

FINISHING: Layer the quilt back, batting, and top; baste all layers together. Outline-quilt around the appliqué pieces, adding additional quilting as desired. The quilt shown in the photograph on pages 52 and 53 is quilted in a grid of approximately 1-inch squares.

When the quilting is complete, trim the quilt layers to measure approximately 75x90 inches. Trim the batting and backing ½ inch smaller than the top. Turn in ¼-inch seam on the top. Fold the hem to the back and hand-sew in place.

Poinsettia Afghan

Shown on page 54.

Finished afghan is 62x73 inches, without fringe.

MATERIALS
Patons Canadiana (3.5-ounce skeins): 19 skeins off-white (104), 2 skeins red (4), 2 skeins green (55), and 1 skein *each* of brown (107) and gold (81)
Size J afghan hook, or size to obtain gauge given below
Size I crochet hook
Tapestry needle

Abbreviations: See page 15.
Gauge: 3½ sts = 1 inch; 3 rows = 1 inch.

INSTRUCTIONS
HOLLY PANEL: (Make three.) With off-white yarn and afghan hook, ch 31.

First half of Row 1: Leaving all lps on hook, sk first ch, * insert hook in next ch, yo, draw up lp; rep from * in each ch across—31 lps on hook.

Second half of Row 1: Yo and draw yarn through first lp on hook, * yo, draw yarn through next 2 lps on hook; rep from * until 1 lp rem on hook.

First half of Row 2: Insert hook under *second* vertical bar, yo, draw up lp and leave on hook; * insert hook in next vertical bar, yo, draw up lp; rep from * across row to within 1 bar of end; insert hook under last bar and thread behind it, yo, draw up lp—31 lps on hook.

Second half of Row 2: Rep Second half of Row 1. Rep Row 2 (first and second halves) until 187 rows are completed.

Last row: Draw up lp under second vertical bar and draw through lp on hook; * draw up lp in next vertical bar and draw through lp on hook; rep from * across to within 1 bar of end; in-

sert hook under last bar and thread behind it, draw up lp and draw through lp on hook; fasten off. Carefully block all panels.

POINSETTIA PANEL: Repeat instructions for the holly panel above, except ch 50—50 lps on hook.

Cross-stitching the holly panels
Use tapestry needle and appropriate yarn colors to cross-stitch

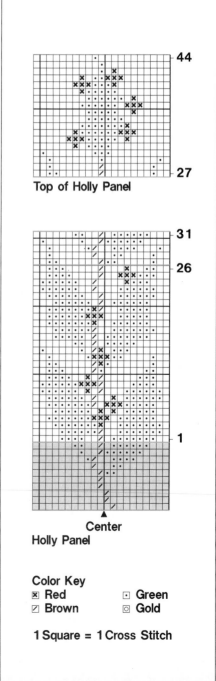

Top of Holly Panel

Center
Holly Panel

Color Key
⊠ Red   ⊡ Green
☑ Brown   ◎ Gold

1 Square = 1 Cross Stitch

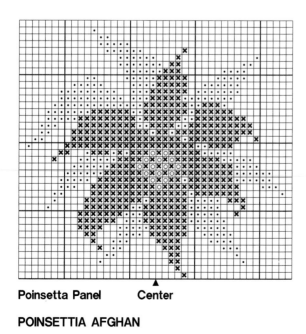

Poinsetta Panel   **Center**

POINSETTIA AFGHAN

the holly leaves on the holly panels. Begin the first row of the holly panel chart, *opposite,* on the sixth row of one holly panel and work the bottom 10 (shaded) rows first, then work rows 1–31 four times plus 1–26 one time. Work the last 18 rows (rows 27–44) to complete the top of the panel. Cross-stitch the remaining two panels.

Cross-stitching the poinsettia panel

Use tapestry needle and appropriate yarn color to cross-stitch the poinsettia panel. Begin the first row of the poinsettia panel chart, *opposite,* on the ninth row of the poinsettia panel. Stitch one poinsettia motif, skip the next eight rows of the panel, then stitch another poinsettia. Continuing as established, stitch two more poinsettias.

EDGING: With Size I crochet hook and off-white, sc evenly spaced around each panel, working a sc in the end sts of each row and 3 scs in each corner. Join with sl st to beg sc, ch 1, do not turn.

Rnd 1: Working in same st as joining, **(yo, pull up lp) 3 times, yo and draw through all 7 lps on hook, yo and draw through 1 lp–puff st made.** Sk sc, sl st in next sc; * puff st in same st as sl st, sk sc, sl st in next sc; rep from * around. Join with sl st. Ch 1, do not turn.

Rnd 2: 2 sc in same st as joining, * 2 sc in next sp between puff sts; rep from * around, working 3 sc in center st of each corner. Sl st to join. Ch 2, do not turn.

Rnd 3: Hdc in each sc around, working 3 hdcs in center st of each corner. Sl st to join, fasten off.

FINISHING: With right sides facing, and referring to photo on page 54 for panel placements, sl st panels together through matching hdcs. Take care not to pull sl sts too tightly to avoid puckering the seams.

With I crochet hook, hdc in each hdc around, working 3 hdcs in center st of each corner and 1 hdc in each joined seam. Sl st to join; fasten off.

For the fringe, cut off-white yarn into 19-inch lengths. With two strands doubled in half, loop and tie fringe in each st across each end. Trim evenly.

Block panels and seams lightly.

Miniature Poinsettia Quilt

Shown on page 55.

Quilt is 24x28 inches.

MATERIALS
1 yard Christmas print cotton fabric for the border
½ yard dark green cotton fabric
¼ yard *each* of deep red and cream cotton fabrics
⅛ yard off-white cotton fabric
1 yard fabric for quilt back
1 yard quilt batting
Cardboard or plastic for templates
DMC embroidery floss: 7 skeins of olive drab (No. 524) and 1 skein of red (No. 304) *or* colors that complement the fabrics you choose
Off-white thread for piecing squares
Gray-green thread for quilting
Water-erasable marker
Embroidery and quilting needles
Embroidery hoop

INSTRUCTIONS
Trace and make cardboard or plastic templates for the poinsettia leaf and flower patterns on page 61. The patterns include a 3/16-inch seam allowance. The dashed line on the patterns indicate the finished size.

TO CUT AND MAKE THE APPLIQUÉ PIECES: Using a double thickness of green fabric (right sides together) and leaf template, trace and cut 12 sets of leaves.

Using a double thickness of red fabric (right sides together) and flower template, trace and cut 12 sets of flowers.

Using coordinating thread, machine-stitch a 3/16-inch seam allowance around *each* of the double thicknesses of the appliqué pieces. Slit the backs of both the green and red appliqué pieces; turn inside out, clip curves, and press.

APPLIQUÉ BLOCKS: *Note:* The remaining quilt pieces include ¼-inch seam allowances.

Cut twelve 3½-inch squares from the off-white fabric. Cut twenty 3½-inch squares from the cream-colored fabric.

Referring to the Appliqué Diagram on page 61, center the leaf shapes (shown in gray on the diagram) on each of the off-white squares and baste into place. Baste the red flower shapes in place over the green leaf shapes. Appliqué-stitch the leaves and flowers using matching thread colors.

PIECING: Alternating squares, and referring to the Piecing Diagram on page 60, sew two sets of *each* of the three strip sets. Begin and end each set with a cream-colored square. Press all seams toward the off-white squares. Sew the strips together, right sides facing. Attach an additional C block to the two corners at the end of each Strip 1. These two blocks are patterned in gray on the Piecing Diagram.

After all strips and blocks have been joined, use a straight edge to mark and cut off excess fabric (indicated as a broken line on the Piecing Diagram). The rectangle should measure 13¾x18 inches. Press.

continued

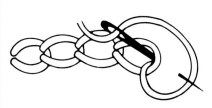

CHAIN-STITCH DIAGRAM

A GARDEN OF POINSETTIAS

BORDERS: From green fabric, cut two 1x24-inch strips, two 1x28-inch strips, two 2x28-inch strips, and two 2x32-inch strips.

From the Christmas print fabric, cut two 5x24-inch strips and two 5x28-inch strips.

Pair the 1x24-inch green strips with the 5x24-inch print strips, and the 1x28-inch green strips with the 5x28-inch print strips. Sew these paired strips together.

With the green portion of the border lined up with the raw edges of the pieced rectangle, center and sew the 24-inch strips to the short sides of the rectangles; then sew the 28-inch strips to the long sides.

Note: The borders on the sample shown on page 55 are of a striped fabric that is mitered at each corner to match the stripes. To miter the fabric at the corners, use an artist's plastic triangle to mark a 45-degree-angle line across each end of the border strip. (The point of the triangle should aim to the center of the cream triangles in the corners of the pieced rectangle.) This 45-degree angle is the sewing line. Carefully match fabrics and sew a seam from inner to outer edge of the border. Trim seam allowance to ¼ inch; press. Repeat the mitering on the border strips for the remaining three corners.

QUILTING: Trace the paisley pattern from the Quilting Diagram, *opposite,* onto tracing paper. Tape the traced pattern onto a sunny window; position and trace pattern onto all cream-colored squares and partial blocks (edge "C" triangles) of the pieced rectangle using the water-erasable marker.

Cut backing fabric and batting into 25x29-inch rectangles. Layer backing, batting, and top pieces together. Baste all layers together.

Using an embroidery hoop to hold fabric taut, and referring to the Appliqué Diagram, *opposite,* work chain stitches (see diagram on page 59) using three strands of olive drab floss to outline the pattern shapes.

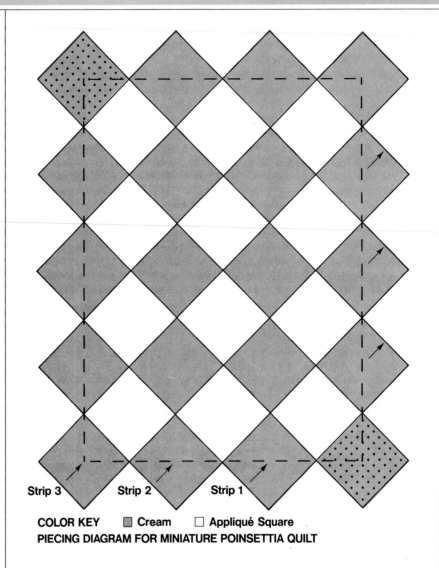

COLOR KEY ■ Cream □ Appliqué Square
PIECING DIAGRAM FOR MINIATURE POINSETTIA QUILT

Make three French knots in the center of each flower using three strands of red floss. Refer to the French Knot Diagram on page 56 to work this stitch.

When all appliquéd squares have been embroidered, quilt all cream-colored blocks and partial blocks using the gray-green quilting thread. Hand- or machine-quilt the border as desired. The model shown on page 55 was quilted along the horizontal lines on the border fabric.

FINISHING: Center and sew the two 2x28-inch green strips to the short sides, allowing the edges to hang over. Sew the remaining two 2x32-inch strips to the long sides, allowing the edges to overlap. Miter corners as before.

Turn and pin green strips to the back so that approximately ½ inch of the green outer border shows on the quilt front. Neatly hand-sew green border to the back.

Remove all basting stitches. Press.

To hang, add a 2½-inch-wide fabric pocket to run the width of the hanging (in the direction of your choice). Turn under all four edges, then hand-stitch both long edges to the back of the hanging, taking care that the stitching does not show on the quilt top. Run a dowel rod through the pocket to hang.

Leaf template

Poinsettia flower template

Quilting diagram

Appliqué diagram

MINIATURE POINSETTIA QUILT
Full-Size Patterns

FESTIVE GIFTS

TO ENJOY YEAR-ROUND

Who can resist a gift that's been fashioned by hand and crafted with pleasure? Not only does it express your love and appreciation on Christmas day, but a handmade gift serves as a reminder of your sentiments the whole year through. This season, give someone you love something you've made from this collection of festive gifts.

Carefully pieced and hand-stitched, a quilt is one of the best presents you can give or receive. Aside from its usefulness as a bed covering, a beautifully made quilt brings a special warmth and vitality to any room it decorates. And, anyone who knows the time and effort it takes to create such a treasure certainly will appreciate the thoughtfulness of your gift.

With its lively colors and vibrant design, the Wonder of the World quilt, *left,* is a true work of art you can give with pride to that special someone on your Christmas list. Stitch it with just two simple pattern pieces and two contrasting fabrics.

This quilt—also known as the Drunkard's Path—was worked with solid-color fabrics. But you can create a quilt that's just as striking using a solid and several scrap print fabrics.

For instructions and full-size patterns for this quilt and the other projects in this chapter, turn to page 70.

The masculine appeal of the quilted loon wall hanging, *above*, and the attractive knit afghan, *opposite*, make these perfect projects to stitch for a special gentleman.

And since both projects combine traditional holiday colors with strong accents of black and white, he'll be sure to display his treasure long after Christmas has come and gone.

The afghan measures 50x70 inches and includes loon borders that measure 8 inches deep. Worked on Size 10 knitting needles with worsted-weight yarns, it's a challenging project for those who love to work with multiple yarn colors.

The matching loon wall hanging measures 45x45 inches and features an appliqué center block with pieced tree motifs that are neatly bordered with flying geese patchwork.

Combine weaving with crochet to create the vivid 50x71-inch afghan, *above*. First, use chain and double crochet stitches to create the striped mesh foundation pattern. Then, weave long strands of yarn through the mesh openings to produce a spectacular plaid fabric and fringe.

A year-round table topper, the 24x74-inch table runner, *opposite*, includes an appliqué block of flowering vines nestled between two traditional patchwork patterns—the Christmas star and the bird's nest. This stunning table covering sets the scene for festive entertaining, whatever the celebration.

The Tree of Life and Bobble Afghan, *above,* is a joy to stitch and is sure to be merrily received. This classic 50x68-inch knit afghan is worked back and forth on Size 8 circular needles and edged with reverse single crochet stitches.

A traditional patchwork pattern provided the inspiration for the 55x70-inch Irish Chain Afghan, *opposite.*

This generously sized afghan is crocheted by the square and includes instructions for joining them as you work.

Wonder of the World Quilt

Shown on pages 62 and 63.

Finished block is 6 inches square. Quilt is 75x87 inches.

MATERIALS
6 yards of green fabric
5½ yards of pink fabric
5 yards of backing fabric
Quilt batting
Quilting thread and needle
Cardboard or plastic for
    templates

INSTRUCTIONS
    Trace and make cardboard or plastic templates for patterns A and B, *right*. Transfer the hatch marks that denote the center of the curves for each template. When tracing the templates onto the fabric, transfer hatch marks again.

    CUTTING THE PIECES: From the green fabric, cut a 1½-yard length and set it aside for the binding. For the pink borders, cut two 2x78-inch strips and two 2x90-inch strips. These measurements include seam allowances and will be trimmed to length when added to the quilt.
    Trace around each template, then add ¼-inch seam allowances before cutting pieces from fabric. (Patterns A and B are finished sizes.)
    Cut 336 *each* of patterns A and B from both remaining fabrics.

    PIECING THE BLOCKS: Stitch together green A pieces and pink B pieces along the curved edges to form 336 pieced squares. Take care to align the center curve markings. Referring to the piecing Block X diagram, *right*, stitch together groups of four pieced squares to make 84 units of Block X.
    Referring to the piecing Block Y diagram, *right,* repeat for all the pink A and green B pieces, joining groups of four pieced squares to make 84 of Block Y.

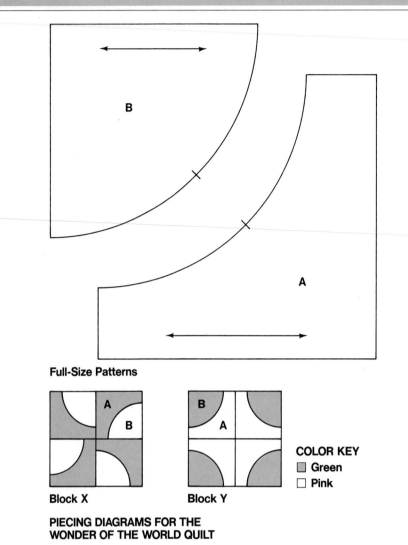

Full-Size Patterns

Block X

Block Y

COLOR KEY
■ Green
□ Pink

PIECING DIAGRAMS FOR THE WONDER OF THE WORLD QUILT

    QUILT ASSEMBLY: Make seven horizontal rows by sewing together six of Block X and six of Block Y. Begin with an X block and alternate the block units. In the same fashion, make seven horizontal rows beginning with a Y block.
    Stitch rows together, alternating the two rows.
    Sew the shorter pink borders to the top and bottom of the quilt; trim excess length even with the quilt. Sew the longer pink borders to the sides of the quilt; trim.

    FINISHING: Cut backing fabric into two equal lengths of 2½ yards each; split one length in half lengthwise. Matching selvage edges and taking ½-inch seams, sew a half panel to each side of the full panel. Trim seams to ¼ inch; press to one side.
    Layer quilt back, batting, and top; baste all three layers together, working out from the center. Quilt ¼ inch from all seams.
    From reserved 1½ yard of green fabric, cut and piece together approximately 10 yards of 3-inch-wide strips for binding. Binding may be cut either on the straight of the fabric grain or on the bias. Press binding in half so it is 1½ inches wide. Match raw edges and right sides of binding and quilt top; machine-stitch through all layers all around quilt. Trim excess batting and backing. Turn the folded edge of binding to the quilt back; blindstitch in place.

Loon Afghan

Shown on page 64.

Afghan measures 50x70 inches.

MATERIALS

Laines anny blatt No. 6 d'anny blatt (50-gram ball): 19 balls ecru (2273), 17 balls black (2272), 5 balls red (2265), and 2 balls green (2219)
Size 10 circular 36-inch knitting needles
Yarn bobbins
Tapestry needle
Stitch markers

Abbreviations: See page 15.
Gauge: 9 sts = 2 inches; 10 rows = 2 inches.

INSTRUCTIONS

With red yarn, cast on 221 sts; do not join. Work in garter st (k every row) for 1¾ inches; fasten off red.

Row 1 (right side): K 8 with black, place marker; join ecru and k 205, place marker; join separate ball of black, k 8.

Note: Slip the markers as you work each row. The markers separate the eight black border sts on both sides of the afghan from the center 205 sts.

Row 2 (wrong side): K 8 with black; p 205 with ecru; k 8 with black.

Row 3: K 8 with black; k 205 with ecru; k 8 with black.

Rows 4-8: Rep rows 2 and 3. End with a Row 2.

Wind four black and four green bobbins to begin to work the loon border. Carry the ecru yarn across the back of the afghan as you work. When changing yarn colors always twist the new color around the color in use to prevent holes.

Row 9: K 8 with black; begin to work from Chart 1, *above top,* as follows: K between A–B once; k between C–B three times; k 8 with black.

Row 10: K 8 with black; p between B–C 4 times; p between C–A once; k 8 with black.

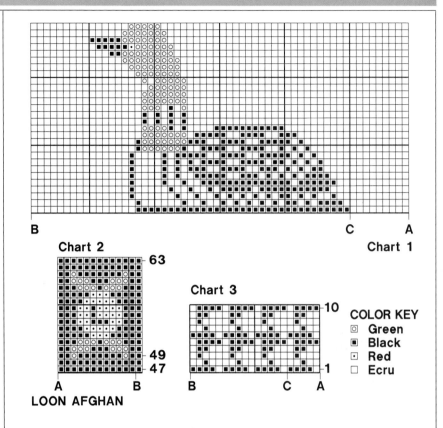

B   **C**   **A**

Chart 1

Chart 2 — 63 / 49 / 47

A   **B**

LOON AFGHAN

Chart 3 — 10 / 1

B   **C**   **A**

COLOR KEY
◙ Green
▣ Black
⊡ Red
☐ Ecru

Rows 11–36: Continue to work pattern from Chart 1, working the 8 black garter sts at each end and the center 205 sts in st sts following the stitching sequence as established in rows 9 and 10.

Row 37: K 8 with black; k 205 with ecru; k 8 with black.

Row 38: K 8 with black; p 205 with ecru; k 8.

Rows 39–44: Rep rows 37 and 38; fasten off ecru at end of Row 44.

Row 45: K 8 with black; join red and k 205; k 8 with black.

Row 46: Rep Row 45 (purl ridge will form on right side of work); fasten off red.

Row 47: Begin to work from Chart 2, *above,* and k all sts with black.

Row 48: With black k 8; p 205; k 8.

Row 49: Wind bobbins with red and green yarns; k 8 with black; continuing to work from Chart 2, k 1 with black, rep between A–B 17 times; k 8 with black.

Row 50: K 8 with black; continue to work from Chart 2 and p between B–A 17 times, p 1 with black; k 8 with black.

Rows 52–61: Continue to work Chart 2, working 8 black garter sts at each end and working center 205 sts in st sts following stitching sequence for rows 49 and 50; fasten off red and green yarn bobbins at end of last row.

Row 62: With black k 8; p 205; k 8.

Row 63: With black k all sts.

Row 64: K 8 with black; join red and p 205; k 8 with black.

Row 65: K 8 with black; p 205 with red (ridge forms on right side of work); k 8 with black; fasten off red.

Row 66: Rep Row 62.

Row 67: K 8 with black; carrying yarn across the back as you work, begin to work Row 1 of Chart 3, *above.* K between A–B 10 times, k from A–C once; k 8 with black.

Row 68: K 8 with black; slip marker; work Row 2 of Chart 3 and p from C–A once, p from B–A 10 times, slip marker; k 8 with black.

Rows 69–76: Continue to work rows 3–10 of Chart 3, working 8 black garter sts at each end and
continued

working center 205 sts in st sts following stitching sequence for rows 67 and 68.

Rep rows 1-10 of Chart 3 until afghan measures approximately 57 inches, ending with Row 10 of chart; fasten off ecru at end of last row.

Next row: Rep Row 63.

Next 2 rows: K 8 with black; join red, k 205 (purl ridge); k 8 with black.

Next 17 rows: Working in reverse order (from Row 63 to Row 47), work Chart 2 following stitching sequence as cited in rows 49 and 50.

Next 2 rows: K 8 with black; k 205 sts with red; k 8 with black.

Next 8 rows: Keeping to black garter sts over 8 border sts, work center 205 sts in st sts with ecru.

Next 28 rows: Working in reverse order, rep Chart 1.

Next 8 rows: Keeping to black garter sts over 8 border sts, work center 205 sts in st sts with ecru; fasten off ecru and black yarns.

Join red and k every row until red border measures 1¾ inches; bind off.

Weave in ends. Block.

Quilted Loon Wall Hanging

Shown on page 65.

Wall hanging is 45 inches square.

Materials
1 yard white fabric
¾ yard of green solid fabric
⅜ yard of red print fabric
¼ yard of green print fabric
16-inch squares *each* of three different gray fabrics
16-inch squares *each* of three different black fabrics
½ yard black fabric (includes binding)
1¾ yards *each* of batting and backing fabric
Thread; needle; ruler; pencil
Rotary cutter and mat (optional)

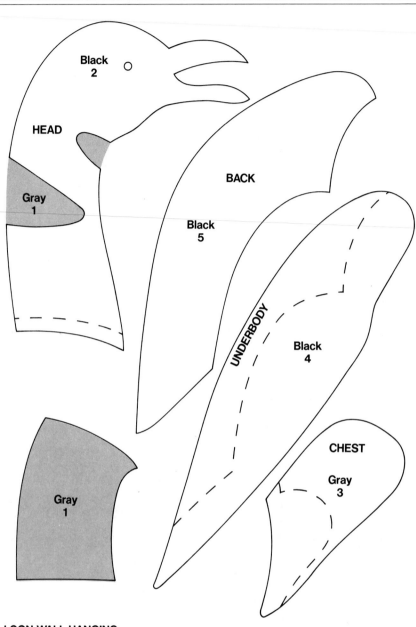

LOON WALL HANGING
Full-Size Patterns

INSTRUCTIONS

A ¼-inch seam allowance is used throughout. All sewing is done with right sides of fabric facing unless otherwise specified.

This design can be made in the traditional manner with 2½-inch (finished size) squares and triangles. However, these instructions describe a quick and easy method to machine-stitch accurate, pieced triangles. The resulting triangle-square units include the necessary seam allowances.

CUTTING THE PIECES: *Note:* Yardage given is sufficient to cut the pieces listed if the fabric is at least 42 inches wide. Cut the following pieces for the different sections of the quilt.

For the large tree blocks

From green print fabric, cut four 3-inch squares. Cut two 5⅞-inch squares; cut these squares in half diagonally to make four triangles.

From the white fabric, cut two

16-inch squares and twelve 3-inch squares. Cut two 3¾-inch squares; cut these squares in quarters diagonally to create eight triangles.

From green solid fabric, cut two 16-inch squares and four 3-inch squares. Cut two 3¾-inch squares; cut these squares in quarters diagonally to create eight triangles.

For the corner tree blocks

From the green print fabric, cut four 1½-inch squares. Cut two 2⅞-inch squares; cut these squares in half diagonally to create four triangles.

From the white fabric, cut two 10½-inch squares and sixteen 1½-inch squares. Cut two 2¼-inch squares; cut these squares in quarters diagonally to make eight triangles.

From green solid fabric, cut two 10½-inch squares and four 1½-inch squares. Cut two 2¼-inch squares; cut these squares in quarters diagonally to make eight triangles.

For the flying geese units

To make the flying geese units, use the three 16-inch gray squares and the three 16-inch black squares. Cut one 16-inch square *each* from the white fabric and the black fabric.

For the borders

From the remaining black fabric, cut seven 2x27-inch strips for the binding, then cut four 4-inch squares for the center border blocks.

Cut eight white 3⅜-inch squares for the center border blocks; cut each in half diagonally to make 16 white triangles.

For the inner border, from the red print, cut two strips 3x31 inches long and two strips 3x36 inches long.

For the appliqué square

Cut one 10½-inch square of white. Reserve scraps of black and gray fabrics for the loon.

ASSEMBLY OF THE LARGE TREE BLOCKS: Lay one large white 16-inch square flat, wrong

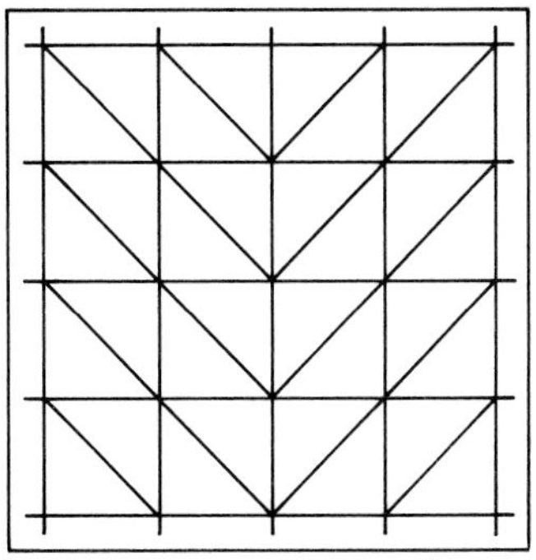

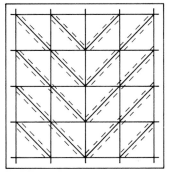

Figure 1

Figure 2

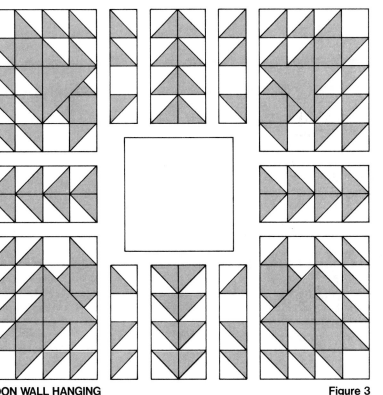

LOON WALL HANGING

Figure 3

side up. With pencil and ruler, mark horizontal and vertical center lines on the fabric. Working out from the center, mark a grid of sixteen 3⅜-inch squares as shown in Figure 1, *top left*. Next, draw diagonal lines through the squares. (Notice how the diagonal lines go in opposite directions. If you've drawn your grid carefully, each diagonal line will intersect through every grid corner.)

Match the marked white square with a green 16-inch square, and with right sides together, pin at corners.

Referring to Figure 2, *top right*, machine-stitch ¼-inch seams on *both* sides of every diagonal line. When all seams are sewn, cut the pieces apart, cutting atop *every* drawn line. You will have two triangle-square units from each grid square drawn.

Repeat with the remaining pair of white and green 16-inch squares to make a total of 64 triangle units. Press seams toward darker fabric.

Using the 64 triangles, and referring to Figure 3, *above,* piece four tree blocks. Leave one side of each block off as illustrated; set blocks aside.

continued

ASSEMBLY OF THE CORNER TREE BLOCKS: Mark and sew a grid of 1⅞-inch squares on the 10½-inch blocks in the same manner as described for the large tree blocks. Assemble corner tree blocks in the same way, except assemble the complete tree. It is not necessary to leave one side off these smaller tree blocks.

ASSEMBLY OF THE FLYING GEESE UNITS: Each flying geese rectangle is made by sewing two triangle-square units together.

Mark the wrong side of each gray 16-inch square with the same grid as described for the large tree blocks. Pair the four black fabric squares with the three gray squares and one white square. Stitch and cut the grids on all four pairs to make 128 triangle-square units. *Note:* For these units, separate the triangle-square units cut from each side of the center *vertical* line of the grid. Match units from each side of the line; the fabric prints all will go in the same direction and will keep "geese" uniform.

You can make either a light goose or a dark goose from each fabric combination, giving you the possibility of eight different combinations. Make some of each, but not an equal number—this random variety gives the wall hanging a "scrappy" look.

WALL HANGING ASSEMBLY: Lay out the assembled pieces for the center of the wall hanging as shown in Figure 3 on page 73. Sew sections together into strips, then assemble the three strips.

APPLIQUÉING THE LOON: Trace the loon shapes on page 72 onto scraps of gray and black fabrics. Add seam allowances and cut shapes from fabric. Turn under seam allowances and press. Referring to the photograph on page 65, pin the loon pieces in place on the white center square. The placement of these pieces is marked by dashed lines on the pattern pieces. Lay the pieces down in numerical order as marked on each pattern.

Align the bottom of the loon with the seam that joins the bottom tree blocks to the side flying geese rectangles. Appliqué each loon piece in place. It is not necessary to stitch an edge that is covered by another piece. Referring to the stitch diagram on page 56, make the loon's eye with a French knot using three strands of red embroidery floss.

INNER BORDER: Sew short red border strips to top and bottom of completed inner section. Trim excess length. Sew remaining red strips at sides.

OUTSIDE BORDER: Sew the long side (hypotenuse) of each white triangle to one side of the black 4-inch squares to make the four center border blocks. Arrange the corner tree blocks, center blocks, and flying geese units in a pleasing manner around the center section. The "geese" all can fly in the same direction, or in opposite directions from the center as in the wall hanging pictured on page 65.

Assemble geese and center squares for top and bottom borders; sew borders to center section. Assemble the side borders, adding corner tree blocks at ends. Sew the side borders onto the wall hanging.

QUILTING: Cut and piece the backing fabric to make a back piece approximately 48 inches square. Lay backing flat, wrong side up, with batting on top of it. Center the top over the batting. Baste the three layers together, working out from the center. Quilt any design you like, using matching or contrasting quilting thread. Remove basting when quilting is complete. Trim batting and backing even with quilt.

BINDING THE QUILT: Stitch the seven binding strips together, end to end, to make one strip approximately 187 inches long. Press the strip in half lengthwise, wrong sides together. Starting at any corner, match the raw edges of the binding strip with the edge of the quilt. Machine-stitch through all layers to the opposite corner. Cut binding even with quilt edge. Repeat on opposite side of quilt. Turn binding over the raw edge and hand-stitch in place on the back. Repeat the binding on the remaining opposite sides of the wall hanging, turning an extra ½ inch of binding to the back at corners.

Festive Table Runner

Shown on page 67.

Table runner measures approximately 24x74 inches

MATERIALS
2⅛ yard of striped fabric
¾ yard of beige print fabric
⅝ yard muslin
½ yard of dark green print fabric for bias strips
½ yard of solid rust fabric for binding and appliqué petals and buds
¼ yard of medium green print fabric for patchwork blocks
¼ yard of burgundy fabric for patchwork blocks
⅛ yard (or scraps) *each* of red paisley and light red print fabrics for appliqué petals
Scraps of green print fabrics for appliqué leaves
1½ yards *each* of batting and backing fabric
Cardboard or template plastic
Quilting thread in matching or contrasting color(s)
Rotary cutter and mat (optional)

INSTRUCTIONS
Note: All seam allowances are ¼ inch wide. Sew all seams with right sides together unless otherwise stated.

CUTTING THE STRIPS AND THE CENTER APPLIQUÉ: From striped fabric, cut two border strips *each* 3½x76 inches and two strips *each* 3½x26 inches. From rust fabric, cut five 2-inch-wide strips across the width of the fabric for binding. From beige print, cut one 13-inch-wide piece down the length of the fabric for the center appliqué. Also from the beige print, cut four 2x19-inch lengthwise strips and two 2x16-inch strips for the sashing. Set the remaining fabric aside for patchwork. Cut one 19x34-inch piece of muslin.

FOR THE CHRISTMAS STAR BLOCK: From medium green fabric, cut four 3-inch squares and two 6¼-inch squares. Cut the larger squares in quarters diagonally to make eight triangles.

From beige print, cut four 3-inch squares, four 2¼-inch squares, and two 3⅜-inch squares. Cut the last two squares in half diagonally to make four triangles.

From burgundy fabric, cut four 4¾-inch squares. Cut each square in quarters diagonally to make a total of 16 triangles.

Trace Pattern A on page 77 onto template material. From striped fabric, cut four pieces. Then cut four pieces of Pattern A reversed. Cut one 4-inch square from any red print fabric for the block center.

Referring to the Christmas Star Block Diagram on page 76, sew the four pairs of Pattern A together, matching stripes. In each pair, set in one 2½-inch beige square. Sew green triangles along the striped sides of the assembled squares to complete one unit (the light gray area). Make three more units.

To assemble the units that are shown in dark gray on the diagram, sew a burgundy triangle onto one side of each medium green square. Sew a red triangle onto two opposite sides of each beige square. Sew remaining red triangles onto beige triangles as illustrated. Matching the seam lines, assemble the three sections into one unit (shaded dark gray). Assemble three more dark gray units.

Sew two dark gray units to opposite sides of the center square.

Lay out all completed units to match the block diagram. Sew two light gray units to each side of the two dark gray units. Matching seams at center, assemble the three pieced units to make a 15½-inch block.

continued

Bud
Cut 4

Tulip
Cut 2

Bud section
Cut 4

Small leaf
Cut 4

Large leaf
Cut 4
Cut 4 reverse

Small flower
Cut 2

First section
large flower
Cut 4

Cut 4 reverse

Second section
large flower
Cut 4

Center of
large flower
Cut 4

FESTIVE TABLE RUNNER
Full-Size Patterns

FOR THE BIRD'S NEST BLOCK: From the beige print fabric, cut nine 2⅝-inch squares. From the striped fabric, cut two 6⅞-inch squares; cut each striped square in half diagonally to make four triangles.

From red paisley fabric, cut two 3⅞-inch squares. From medium green print fabric, cut six 3⅞-inch squares.

Cut each red and green square in half diagonally to make four red and 12 green triangles.

From burgundy fabric, cut two 4¼-inch squares. Cut each into quarters diagonally to make eight triangles. Cut ten 2⅝-inch squares. Cut each in half diagonally to make 20 triangles.

Assemble four light gray units as shown on the Bird's Nest Block Diagram, *below,* and four dark gray units. Piece the remaining four burgundy triangles and beige square to assemble the center square block. Assemble the pieced units to make a 15½-inch block.

APPLIQUÉD CENTER BLOCK: Fold the 19x34-inch muslin rectangle in half vertically; press to mark center. Unfold and fold the piece in half horizontally; press to mark centers, then unfold.

With the ruler, measure along the vertical line 5¾ inches in each direction from the center to mark top and bottom points of the oval. Measure 11¼ inches on each side of the horizontal line to mark side points of the oval. Sketch out the oval, connecting the points. Cut out the oval.

Turn under and press ¼-inch seam allowance of oval. Center and baste the oval atop the beige print rectangle.

Referring to the bias strip tip box on page 25, make a continuous bias strip ⅜ inch wide from green print fabric.

Referring to the Appliqué Block Diagram, *below,* cut two 7½-inch lengths (marked in pink) of bias and baste the ends at center of one side. Cut a 30-inch length of bias and pin around oval, following the gray lines on the diagram and covering the raw edges of the first two strips. Pin the first two shorter pieces in place, curving in opposite directions out of the oval toward the corners of the muslin. Where they cross, the shorter pieces should lie over the longer strip.

Cut two 6-inch bias stems (marked in pink) and insert them under the long bias; pin in place.

Turn the block around and pin bias stems to the opposite side in a mirror-image position. Hand-appliqué all stems in place.

Trace leaf and flower shapes on page 75 onto template plastic; cut

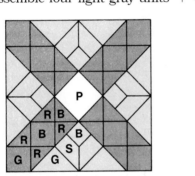

CHRISTMAS STAR BLOCK

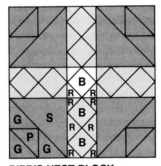

BIRD'S NEST BLOCK

P = Red Paisley or Print   B = Beige Print   R = Burgundy
G = Medium Green   S = Striped

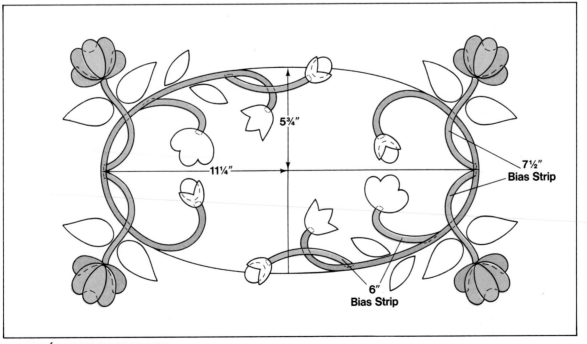

**APPLIQUÉ BLOCK DIAGRAM FOR
THE FESTIVE TABLE RUNNER**

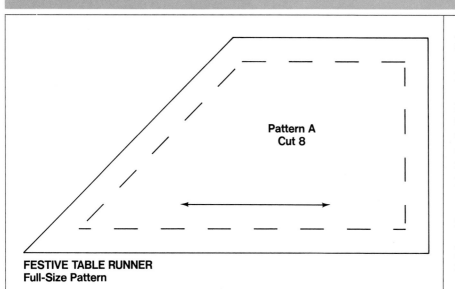

FESTIVE TABLE RUNNER
Full-Size Pattern

(within pattern diagram: **Pattern A** / **Cut 8**)

out plastic shapes. Trace templates onto wrong sides of appropriate fabrics, leaving room between tracings to add seam allowances. Cut out shapes, adding a scant 3/16-inch seam allowance.

Turn under seam allowances, clipping curves and points to obtain nice shapes. Press lightly. Referring to the Appliqué Block Diagram, pin each shape in position and appliqué in place.

Remove visible basting from the oval edge; appliqué muslin to the remaining edges of oval. Trim the muslin to 18½x32½ inches.

SASHING: Sew short sashing strips to the sides of both pieced blocks. Trim sashing even with blocks. Sew remaining strips to top and bottom of blocks; trim excess length. Each block should measure 18½ inches square. Sew one block to each end of the appliquéd center.

BORDERS: Mitering the corners, sew the short border strips to runner ends and then the longer strips to the sides.

QUILTING: Layer backing, batting, and runner top; baste all three layers together. Quilt any design you like. The table runner shown on page 67 features outline quilting ¼ inch inside each seam line and parallel gridded lines in the center section. When

quilting is complete, trim batting and backing even with top.

BINDING: Seam all five binding strips end to end to make one strip approximately 2x210 inches long. Press strip in half lengthwise, wrong sides together.

Starting at one corner, match raw edges of binding to one long side of the quilt. Machine-stitch ¼ inch from the edge through all layers. Cut binding even with edge. Repeat on opposite side. Turn binding over raw edge and hand sew in place on backing. Sew binding on remaining sides; trim excess, leaving ½ inch extra at ends. Fold excess down, then fold binding over raw edge to the back and hand-stitch in place.

Plaid Afghan

Shown on page 66.

Afghan measures 50x71 inches.

MATERIALS
Aarlan Royal Tweed (50-gram skeins): 13 skeins red (1346), 7 skeins *each* of black (1348) and off-white (1303)
Size I crochet hook, or size to obtain gauge given below
Large-eye tapestry needle

Abbreviations: See page 15.
Gauge: 8 mesh = 4 inches.

INSTRUCTIONS
The entire agfhan is crocheted in an open mesh pattern in assorted bands of color. When the crocheting is completed, strands of yarn are woven through the mesh openings to create the plaid.

AFGHAN: Using red yarn ch 220.
Row 1: Dc in sixth ch from hook, * ch 1, sk ch, dc in next ch; rep from * across; ch 4, turn—108 sps.
Row 2: Sk first dc, * dc in next dc, ch 1; rep from * across; end ch 1, sk ch of turning ch, dc in next ch; ch 4, turn.
Rep Row 2 twice more—4 rows of red. Continue to work mesh pattern as established changing colors as follows: * work 2 rows of off-white, 2 rows of black, 4 rows of red, 2 rows of black, 2 rows of off-white, and 4 rows of red; rep from * until crocheted piece measures 71 inches.

WEAVING: Use three strands of yarn, *each* cut 92 inches long, threaded on a tapestry needle to weave the yarn through the mesh. Weave the yarns lengthwise under and over the mesh bars. Alternate the under and over weavings on each succeeding row so the strands interlock and create a fabric texture.

Mark the vertical center of the afghan (there will be 54 mesh bands on each side of middle). Weave in the spaces from the right of middle as follows: 2 bands of red, * 2 bands of off-white, 2 bands of black, 4 bands of red, 2 bands of black, 2 bands of off-white, 4 bands of red, rep from * 3 times more; end with 2 bands of off-white and 2 bands of black. Weave the left side following the same directions beginning with 2 bands of red.

Weave in ends. Block carefully. Trim fringe evenly across top and bottom of afghan.

Irish Chain Afghan

Shown on page 69.

Afghan measures 55x70 inches.

MATERIALS
Coats & Clark Red Heart 4-ply knit and crochet yarn (3.5 ounce skein): 10 skeins grass green (675) A, 6 skeins country red (914) B, and 5 skeins tan (334) C
Size I crochet hook or size to obtain gauge given below
Tapestry needle

Abbreviation: See page 15.
Gauge: Each small block is a 2¼-inch square.

INSTRUCTIONS
Note: Directions for this afghan include instructions for assembling the blocks into the afghan as you complete the last round of each square. You also can make the squares separately, then sew or crochet them together when all the squares are completed. If you choose to make this afghan using the latter method, you'll need to crochet 210 small squares with green, 160 small squares with red, and 40 large squares with tan. Refer to the chart, *right,* for color placement when assembling the afghan.

FIRST SMALL SQUARE: With red ch 5, join with sl st to form ring.
Rnd 1: Ch 3 (counts as dc), work 2 dc in ring; * ch 1—for corner, 3 dc in ring; rep from * 2 times more; ch 1, join with sl st to top of beg ch-3. Sl st into next 2 dc and into ch-1 corner sp.
Rnd 2: Ch 3, in same sp work 2 dc, ch 1, 3 dc; * in next ch-1 corner sp work 3 dc, ch 1, and 3 dc; rep from * 2 times more; join with sl st to top of beg ch-3; fasten off.

SECOND SMALL SQUARE (joining square): With green ch 5, join with sl st to form ring.
Rnd 1: Rep Rnd 1 of First Small Square.
Rnd 2: Ch 3, in same sp work 2 dc, ch 1, 3 dc; * in next ch-1 corner sp work 3 dc, sl st in ch-1 corner sp of preceding square, 3 dc in same corner sp of square in progress; sl st in sp between dc-grp of preceding square; working on the square that's in progress, rep between the *s; in next ch-1 corner sp work 3 dc, ch 1, 3 dc; join with sl st to top of beg ch-3; fasten off.
Complete Strip 1 following the instructions for the Second Small Square, working the remaining 18 squares in the appropriate colors and joining them to the preceding square.

Begin to work Strip 2 and work one green square and join it to the top of the first square in Strip 1.

LARGE TAN SQUARE: Ch 5, join with sl st to form ring.
Rnds 1 and 2: Rep rnds 1 and 2 of the First Small Square.
Rnd 3: Sl st into next 2 dc and into ch-1 sp; ch 3, in same sp work 2 dc, ch 1, and 3 dc; * 3 dc in sp between 2 dc-grps; in corner ch-1 sp work 3 dc, ch 1, 3 dc; rep from * 2 times more; 3 dc in sp between next 2 dc-grps; join with sl st to top of beg ch-3.
Rnds 4 and 5: Rep Rnd 3, having one more group of 3 dc on

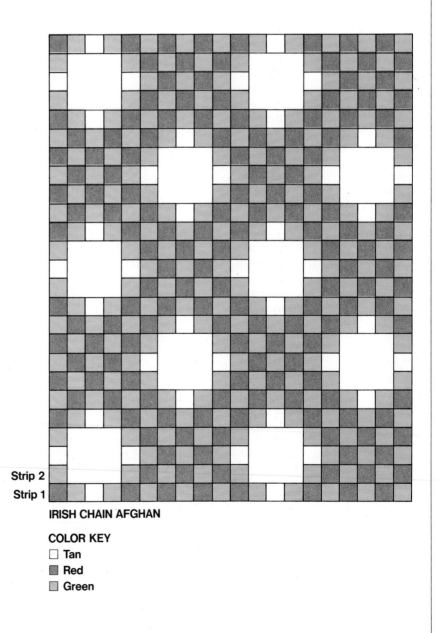

Strip 2
Strip 1

IRISH CHAIN AFGHAN

COLOR KEY
☐ Tan
▨ Red
▨ Green

each side of square—at end of Rnd 4 there are 2 dc-grps on each side; at end of Rnd 5, there are 3 dc-grps on each side.

Rnd 6: Sl st into next 2 dc and into ch-1 sp; ch 3, in same sp work 2 dc, ch 1, 3 dc; (3 dc in sp between next 2 dc-grp) 4 times; in corner ch-1 sp work 3 dc, ch 1, 3 dc; (3 dc in sp between next 2 dc-grp) 3 times; sl st into ch-1 corner sp of green square on Strip 2; 3 dc in sp between next 2 dc-grp on tan square; sl st into sp between next 2 dc-grp on green square; in corner ch-1 sp of tan square work 3 dc, sl st into corner ch-1 of red square; work 3 dc in same corner of tan square; sl st in sp between next 2 dc-grp on green square; 3 dc in next sp on tan square, sl st in *joining sp* between next two small squares; continue to work the sixth rnd of the tan square and join it to the 3 small squares of Strip 1. Complete the remaining side with no joinings; join to top of ch-3 at beg of rnd; fasten off.

Note: When joining squares where four corners come together, always sl st to the square that is *opposite* to the one in progress. When joining the tan square where two small squares are joined, do not work the joinings in the corners, but in the joining sts *between* these two squares.

Continue to make squares, fastening them together on the last rnd of the small or large square. Follow the chart for the color placements of all squares.

BORDER: *Rnd 1:* With right side facing and green yarn, sc around afghan, working 3 sc in each corner; fasten off, turn.

Rnd 2: With wrong side facing and tan yarn, join yarn in any st, ch 2; hdc in each sc around, working hdc, ch 1, and hdc in center sc of each corner; join to top of beg ch-2; do not turn.

Rnds 3 and 4: Ch 2, *working in front lps,* hdc in each hdc around, working 2 hdc, ch 1, and 2 hdc in each ch-1 sp of corner; join to top of beg ch-2. Fasten off at end of Rnd 4.

Rnd 5: Join green in any st, ch 2; working in front lps, hdc in each hdc around, working hdc, ch 1, and hdc in each ch-1 sp of corner; join to top of beg ch-2.

Rnds 6 and 7: Ch 2, working in both lps of st, hdc in each hdc around, working 2 hdc, ch 1, and 2 hdc in each ch-1 sp of corner; join with sl st to top of beg ch-2; ch 2, turn.

Rnd 8: Working from left to right, * sc in hdc, ch 2, sk hdc; rep from * around; join to beg sc; fasten off.

FINISHING: Weave in all ends and block lightly so border and squares lay smoothly.

Tree of Life and Bobble Afghan

Shown on page 68.

Afghan measures 50x68 inches.

MATERIALS
Brunswick Germantown knitting worsted (3.5-oz. skeins): 18 skeins white sand (4001)
36-inch Size 8 circular knitting needle or size to obtain gauge given below
Stitch markers
Cable needle
Size F crochet hook

Abbreviations: See page 15.
Kb: K into back of st.
Rc st (right cross st): With cable needle, sl next st and hold in back of work, k next st, then p st from cable needle.
Lc st (left cross st): With cable needle, sl next st and hold in front of work, p next st, then k st from cable needle.
Gauge: 5.8 sts = 1 inch.

INSTRUCTIONS
BOBBLE PATTERN (worked over 11 sts)
Row 1 (right side): Kb 1, p 1, kb 1, p 5, kb 1, p 1, kb 1.
Row 2: P 1, k 1, p 1, k 5, p 1, k 1, p 1.

Row 3: Kb 1, p 1, kb 1, p 2, **(k in front and back of same st) twice, (turn, p these same 4 sts, turn, k 4) twice, sl second, third, and fourth st over the first st—bobble made;** p 2, kb 1, p 1, kb 1.
Rows 4, 6, 8: Rep Row 2.
Rows 5, 7: Rep Row 1.
Rep these 8 rows for pattern.

TREE OF LIFE PATTERN (worked over 17 sts)
Row 1 (right side): P 7, kb 3, p 7.
Row 2 and all even rows: K the k sts and p the p sts.
Row 3: P 6, rc st, kb 1, lc st, p 6.
Row 5: P 5, rc st, p 1, kb 1, p 1, lc st, p 5.
Row 7: P 4, rc st, p 2, kb 1, p 2, lc st, p 4.
Row 9: P 3, rc st, p 3, kb 1, p 3, lc st, p 3.
Row 11: P 2, rc st, p 4, kb 1, p 4, lc st, p 2.
Row 13: P 1, rc st, p 4, kb 3, p 4, lc st, p 1.
Row 14: Work as for all even rows.
Rep rows 3–14 for pattern. (12 row repeat)

Cast on 293 sts onto circular needles; do not join.
Row 1 (right side): K 1, * work Row 1 of Bobble Pattern over next 11 sts, place marker; work Row 1 of Tree of Life Pattern over next 17 sts, place marker; rep from * 9 times more; work Row 1 of Bobble Pattern over next 11 sts, k 1.
Row 2: K 1, * work Row 2 of Bobble Pattern over next 11 sts, sl marker; work Row 2 of Tree of Life Pattern over next 17 sts, sl marker; rep from * 9 times more; work Row 2 of Bobble Pattern over next 11 sts, k 1. Continue to work in patterns as established until piece measures 68 inches; bind off in pattern.

FINISHING: With Size F crochet hook, sc evenly spaced around all sides of afghan, working 3 sc in each corner; join with a sl st to first sc. Ch 1, do not turn. Working from left to right (reverse crochet), sc in each sc around; fasten off. Weave in ends and block.

ACKNOWLEDGMENTS

We would like to extend our special thanks to the following designers who contributed projects to this book. When more than one project appears on a page, the acknowledgment cites both the project and the page number. A page number alone indicates one designer contributed all of the projects on that page.

Beth Bohac—9

Marlee Carter—40–41, 65, 67

Jackie H. Curry—41, afghan

Susan Z. Douglas—18–19

Dixie Falls—38–39

Raymond Gustafson—22–23

Carol V. Hall—36–37, 55

Joyce Nordstrom—69

Nancy Reames—6, 21, 54

Valerie Root—64, 66, 68

Helene Rush—7–8

A special thank-you is extended to the following person who loaned us antique quilts for projects.

Shelly Zegart Quilts—4–5, 52–53

We would like to thank the following people whose technical skills are greatly appreciated.

Elizabeth Porter

Margaret Sindelar

Patricia Wilens

For their cooperation and courtesy, we extend a special thanks to the following sources for providing materials for projects.

Aarlan Yarns
24770 Crestview
Farmington Hills, MI 48018
   for afghans on pages 18–19, 66

Anny Blatt Yarns
24770 Crestview
Farmington Hills, MI 48018
   for afghan on page 64

Bernat Yarn and Craft Corp.
Depot and Mendon Sts.
Uxbridge, MA 01569
   for afghan on page 8

Brunswick Yarns
P.O. Box 276
Pickens, SC 29671
   for afghans on pages 6, 22–23, 68

C. M. Offray & Son, Inc.
261 Madison Ave.
New York, NY 10016
   for ribbon on page 21 and assorted gift ribbons

Coats & Clark, Inc.
Dept. C. S., P.O. Box 1010
Toccoa, GA 30577
   for afghan on page 69

Dogwood Lane
Main Street, P.O. Box 145
Dugger, IN 47848
   for buttons on page 21

Hallmark Cards, Inc.
Kansas City, MO 64141
   for gift wraps

Heritage Imports
P.O. Box 328
Pella, IA 50219
   for curtains on pages 22 and 55

Patons Yarn
212 Middlesex Ave.
Chester, CT 06412
   for afghan on page 54

Reynolds Yarn
A division of Johnson Creative Arts
445 Main St.
West Townsend, MA 01474
   for afghan on page 7

We also are pleased to acknowledge the following photographers whose talents and technical skills contributed much to this book.

Hopkins Associates—4–9; 20–22; 36–41; 52–54; 62–69

Scott Little—18–19; 23; 55

Have BETTER HOMES AND GARDENS® magazine delivered to your door. For information, write to:
MR. ROBERT AUSTIN
P.O. BOX 4536
DES MOINES, IA 50336